MW00437222

Invisible, Invincible
Black Women
— Growing Up *in* —
Bronzeville

Portia McClain
Edited with Guy Stewart and Linard Mac

Copyright © 2020 Portia McClain
All rights reserved
First Edition

PAGE PUBLISHING, INC.
Conneaut Lake, PA

First originally published by Page Publishing 2020

ISBN 978-1-6624-2062-7 (pbk)
ISBN 978-1-6624-2063-4 (digital)

Printed in the United States of America

In memory of my mother and all the other women of Bronzeville; to my grandmothers, who taught me common sense and the importance of family; my uncles and aunts; my sister Bernadine and my brother Jeffro; and all my friends who grew up with me and are no longer with us.

To my family members, I love you all.

Portia as a baby with her mom in 1946.

Contents

Acknowledgment

I would like to thank my brother Linard Mac and Guy Stewart, my friend and colleague, for their help and support and for their time and effort in editing this book.

I would like to thank my family for all their support.

Prologue

Many centuries ago, in many African tribes, there was a designated historian or keeper of the family history, known as a griot. The griot would gather people around the fireplace and tell stories of family events, tribal losses and gains, etc., in effect, a talking history of the past. This verbal history was handed down by means of the designated griot through generations of people and family members.

Although modern-day Black Americans have gotten away from the idea of a designated storyteller, the history of our culture is still handed down through generations and stories. The story you will read about is a combination of history that has been handed down to me, along with my eyewitness account of the things I saw. In most cases, there are no names; this work is written in a third-person narrative, but the stories are true as told in our oral history.

Before 1900

I have often heard it said that you must know your past to understand the present to shape your future. I believe that to be true. I knew, growing up, my family's history and where I came from. This enabled me to have a sense of identity and direction. As I tell my story and chronicle my mother's and a few other heroic women's story of Bronzeville, it is important to me to recollect what Black women who were slaves did to protect their men and children and how they suffered at the hands of their White masters. Demeaned, raped, and beaten as my great-grandmothers and great-great-grandmothers were, but despite the horrible life conditions inflicted upon them, they persevered. I know how fortunate I am to have known these great women who had been slaves. Their courage helped me understand where my own mother obtained her strength and I mine with the will to survive.

In the early 1800s, my great-great-grandfather Richard was taken into port at North Carolina from, I assume, Nigeria, Africa. As my DNA shows, I am 43 percent Nigerian, 22 percent European, and 9 percent Native American. My great-great-grandfather was sold as a slave in North Carolina before finally being sold again into South Carolina and then into Mississippi. Richard Payne was the slave name he was given, ignoring the fact that he was a person with a name before his capture and enslavement.

Our oral family-history records say he grew up a freed slave who had highly marketable skills as a blacksmith. The skills gave him special privileges and allowed him to travel and behave as a freed slave.

In North Carolina, there was conflict between the church and the state leaders concerning people who were sympathetic to the plight of the slaves. This led to some slaves being sold into South Carolina and other states. Richard, a free Black man, was recaptured and sold into South Carolina and thus had his freedom taken away. Because he was accustomed to having freedom as a blacksmith, his slave owners saw him as a real and viable threat and a problem to maintaining the security and control of the other slaves.

To eliminate the problem, Richard was sold again in Jackson, Mississippi. The new slave owners encountered the same problems with Richard because he refused to accept the duties of a slave and would run when he had the chance. He was sent to live on a plantation, located about sixty miles south of Jackson, three miles from the Skiffer Church in rural Mississippi, not far from Prentiss, where he and my great-great-grandmother lived on the McLauren Plantation.

While Richard had been a runaway, at times he lived in the camps of the Cherokee. He eventually took a wife who was of a Cherokee tribe. There were no laws permitting such a marriage, and when they were caught again, the two of them and their children were taken into slavery and returned to the plantation. The plantation (slave) owner was a leading steward of Hopewell Presbyterian Church in Skiffer, Mississippi.

The plantation owner allowed his slaves to attend church with him, and after the abolishment of slavery, he helped to organize a church for his newly freed former slaves.

Richard; his wife, Lou; and their children remained on the plantation and homesteaded the land adjoining the plantation in Simpson County, Mississippi, in the mid-1800s. It was also known as the Skiffer Community. It was there he continued his profession as a blacksmith until his death. The land was passed down to my great-grandmother, the youngest of his thirteen slave children; two of the thirteen had been sold off away from the family, never to be seen again. The land was then passed down to my great-grandmother and her husband, and even today, about ten acres of the land is still owned by a member of our family.

Harry and Lou lived on the land and raised their eleven children (seven girls and four boys), one of whom was my grandmother.

My mother and her siblings were sharecroppers on the same land when I was born in the midforties, and they were the children of Mitchell and Della. My grandfather Mitchell would pick me up and carry me around on his neck in the fields as I watched my mother and her siblings pick cotton, and my grandmother and great-grandmother quilted on the porch.

On occasion, I try to visualize what my mother's life may have been like from childhood to early adulthood. By putting together bits and pieces of oral history I was given and heard from relatives, I've assembled this portrait of my mother's life before I was born.

The house my grandparents lived in and my mother grew up in was in Jefferson Davis County, Mississippi, on the McLauren plantation. They inherited this house and the land it stood on from her parents. They lived in the country sixty miles south of Jackson, Mississippi. The description of the house, as I remember as a little girl, had shutters but no glass windows. It was so dark you couldn't see your hand in front of your face; there were no lights in the country. I sometimes fell into the outhouse because of the darkness. An oil lamp provided the only light they had. They did not have running water or indoor plumbing, so they used the outhouse as their bathroom and well water for washing drinking, and bathing. A metal washtub and washboard were used to clean their laundry.

They raised and cured their own meat, planted their own vegetables, cotton, sugarcane, and peanuts and sharecropped the land. Occasionally, you could hear and see the nightriders riding though the country back roads with torches burning, terrorizing the Black people who lived there.

Jean, the Early Years

My mother was born December 3, 1919, in Prentiss, Mississippi. I was told by one of my aunts that, by the time my mother was nine years old, my grandmother and my grandfather could do nothing with her.

She was rebellious, angry, and noncompliant, and no one knew why. They sent her away to an aunt in Ohio, but she only lived there for a short time before she was sent back to Mississippi. They said she hadn't changed at all and no one could do anything with her. Her behavior seemed to get worse as time passed, and my aunts alluded to some deep, dark secret in the family as the reason for her behavior, but they never said what that deep, dark secret was. They left that to my imagination. Women were physically and sexually abused all around me, and my imagination was very vivid, and I immediately thought that could be what happened to my mother.

I recall having to turn in the son of a longtime friend because he was having vaginal and oral sex with his twelve-year-old daughter and discovering that he himself was also sexually molested as a child by an uncle. Some of the ways that people dealt with and tried to escape the issues of the era were entertainment, drugs, prostitution, and gambling.

My mother, Jean, was a complex woman. Although she could be described as complex and conflicted, I saw her as caring, giving, and sharing during my childhood and adulthood. She was always extending a helping hand to anyone. As she grew older and acquired her own home, her door was always open. She was so wise and a beautiful person inside out. I cannot remember her ever telling me anything that didn't come to pass. She could see things and make predictions about life that sometimes you would think were so far-fetched they were unbelievable. Sometimes, she would say things that sounded so far-fetched that, if you didn't see those very things come to pass with your own eyes or hear it with your own ears, you would have thought she was crazy. But she wasn't; she was wise, and she earned it. She was indeed one of a kind, and she lived her life on her own terms regardless of what anyone else thought. Everyone loved "Aint" Jean, and in my opinion, she represented something they wished they had.

Bronzeville and the Migration North

My family came up from Mississippi during the Great Migration, though it was, in fact, the second migration from the South. African Americans leaving the rural South in search of a better way of life, jobs, and housing came with a deep yearning for security and freedom. They brought with them the music of the rural South, called the Delta Blues, and the food of Black people.

Unlike the first migration of the late 1900s through the 1920s and thirties, which yielded the well-to-do Blacks of the Jazz Age, the migration we were part of consisted of poorer folk from the rural South, the sharecroppers.

From the early 1900s to 1960, millions of Blacks migrated from the South to the North to escape oppression, economic hardship, and the Jim Crow laws and in search of a better life. My mom arrived in Chicago in 1944 and landed in a community called Bronzeville, which became our home.

Like Bronzeville, every city has its historical neighborhood, and to the children who grow up there, like me, growing up in that neighborhood was like no other place. Bronzeville, also known as the Black Metropolis, as well as the Harlem of Chicago, was that kind of un-forgettable place for me. It was historical and unforgettable in many ways and for many reasons; some were happy, and some had a lot of sadness.

My memories echoed those put down by Timuel Black, a historian still living in Bronzeville. A longtime resident there, he wrote, "Black folks were more afraid of what they left behind in the South than what they would find in the North."

Life was too hard for my mother and father to accept staying in the South any longer, according to my mother. Yet sometimes I wish they had stayed there. What they found in the North was just as frightening as what they left behind in the South.

Destruction of the Black family system as they and I knew it to be was happening in both places. Sometimes, I think my family would have been better off staying in the South. Maybe some of my family members would still be alive, and my life would have been different in many ways. The lives of those generations to come might have had a better chance at experiencing a better future.

When the migration to the North began, the family unit consisted of a father, a mother, children, and the strong support of grandparents. It never occurred to them, especially the father, that the family would face a situation without ways for him to provide the necessities of life for his family. Prior to the migration up North, Black men and women could sharecrop and hunt for food like possums, squirrels, and rabbits to feed their families. Planting, fishing, hunting, and gathering up what the land yielded were feasible to feed their families. They grew their own vegetables. In the urban North, there were no jobs. Men couldn't plant or hunt, and this inability to provide for their families led to profound frustration and anger. The unvented anger, for many men, led to physical, verbal, and sexual abuse we talked about previously, which ended in broken families and women becoming the matriarchs and leaders of our communities.

The Fame and History of Bronzeville

Growing up in Bronzeville, I saw many famous people living and working there. Some of them I saw at the famous Regal Theater. Frankly, I don't know why the Apollo Theater in Harlem is more popular than the Regal Theater in Bronzeville. According to some researchers, they two sprang up at the same time. New York's Harlem and Chicago's Bronzeville were very much two of the places where Black people were welcome after the migrations from the South, especially Bronzeville. Bronzeville was a place where Black people or other minorities could live, work, and perform, sometimes being the first stop from the South. Anyone who had an art, whether it was music, poetry, writing, or dance, any talent was welcome.

Bronzeville was a place to live and work in at a time of segregation. Some of the same entertainers who performed in Bronzeville traveled between the two cities, performing at the Apollo in New York and the Regal Theater in Chicago. People like comedian Richard Prior; one of the greatest jazz singers of all time, Sarah Vaughn; comedian Bill Cosby; jazz singer Billy Eckstein; and great poets like Gwendolyn Brooks who lived and worked in Bronzeville. Muddy Waters, the most well-known blues singer in America, lived in Bronzeville after migrating from the South. When he passed away, I attended his funeral at the historical Metropolitan Funeral Home, the only Black-owned funeral parlor in Bronzeville and in the city of Chicago. When Dinah Washington, one of the greatest blues singers of all time, passed away, my mother took me to her funeral on the West Side of Chicago at one of the largest historical ballrooms in Chicago, the Aragon Ballroom. Josephine Baker, singer and dancer, came to perform at the Regal Theater for her benefits every summer. I was always in the front row when she came to town because she was an inspiration to me. I had never seen a Black woman who wore Ziegfeld Girls clothing perform like she did. I knew if she, as a Black woman, could do something like that, I could do better and get out of the ghetto.

Her opening act was Brock Peters, an actor who would one day be best known for playing the role of Tom Robinson in the 1962 film *To Kill a Mockingbird*. Richard Wright, an author whose work helped change race relations in the United States in the mid-twentieth century, came to Bronzeville to work. Red Foxx, comedian and actor, lived and worked in Bronzeville. He was also a regular emcee at the Regal Theater and later became the lead actor in the sitcom *Sanford and Son*. The great gospel singer Mahalia Jackson lived and worked in Bronzeville and she sang "Troubles of the World" in the 1959 film *Imitation of Life*, which starred Kim Novak and Sandra Dee. I remember seeing Santana at the Regal and in the neighborhood. Nat King Cole lived about five blocks from where I lived in Bronzeville.

Some celebrities who came to Chicago to perform at the Regal Theater also indulged in the bars scattered throughout Bronzeville and joined others who came to buy their drugs, which created a huge market and demand for drugs and prostitution. The ones who helped to perpetuate poverty in the ghetto were those who brought the drugs in.

Bronzeville had become a cultural center. The Regal, located in the heart of Bronzeville on Chicago's South Side, was a nightclub and music theater. It was a great place, much like the Apollo Theater in New York. The same artists traveled back and forth between the two theaters, but you didn't hear as much about the Regal as you did about the Apollo. Nat "King" Cole, Cab Calloway, Louis Armstrong, Ella Fitzgerald, Sarah Vaughan, Lena Horne, Dinah Washington, Miles Davis, Sammy Davis Jr., Lionel Hampton, Dizzy Gillespie, Duke Ellington, Jackie Wilson, the Supremes, the Temptations, the

Four Tops, Herbie Hancock, Dell Reese, Gladys Knight and the Pips, Lola Falana, Louis Jordan and his Tympany Five, Solomon Burke, International Sweethearts of Rhythm, Dionne Warwick, James Brown and the Famous Flames, the Isley Brothers, John Coltrane, Dorothy Dandridge, Revella Hughes, Five Stairsteps, Peg Leg Bates, Dave Peyton and Martha Reeves and the Vandellas, "Little" Stevie Wonder, Marvin Gaye, Smokey Robinson and the Miracles, Mary Wells, and the Marvelettes, B. B. King, the Jackson 5, Gladys Knight and the Pips, and Bobby Taylor and the Vancouvers. All of them were there at one time or another.

But a lot of people never knew that perhaps because the original Regal closed in 1968 and was finally torn down in 1971. It should have been made a landmark just as the Apollo is now. And yes, I am a bit biased toward it because my life and this book evolved around the Regal Theater. There was something special about Bronzeville and the Regal Theater; growing up there was bittersweet. The Regal was my haven from my world of despair. I was a young girl growing up in a place that could have been a very dangerous place for me.

The irony is, although it was dangerous because of the things we saw and experienced, it was also special, and I was too young to understand how special it was. I sometimes compare my life to that of the famous poet and writer Gwendolyn Brooks, after reading some of her works, like "The Boy Died in My Alley," written in her famous book *A Street in Bronzeville*. Gwendolyn Brooks was poet laureate to Illinois and the Kennedy White House. She has written many children's books that are not being taught in schools to Black children but should be.

I compare myself to her only in that I lived what she wrote about. I understood "The Boy Died in My Alley" because I too saw many boys—and girls—die in my alley. It was exhilarating and comforting that I could identify with someone so famous and accomplished who experienced some of what I experienced. Even though she was older than I was, she stilled lived there during the time I was growing up. It was comforting to know I wasn't the only one to experience Bronzeville in that way. Like me, she also had mixed emotions about the richness of Bronzeville's cultural atmosphere and the artistry of the people of so many different backgrounds and genres, as well as the heroin addicts, organized crime, prostitution, and violence.

My family was migrating from the South just as Gwendolyn Brooks and her family migrated from Kansas City, Missouri.

This area has a long-standing history, and it is important to know some of that history to understand the plight of the African American people who migrated and lived in this community after they migrated to understand the story of the women and children of Bronzeville.

A larger population of German Jews relocated to Bronzeville after their homes were destroyed in the Great Chicago Fire. Dr. Martin Luther King Drive was once called the Grand Boulevard. At Twenty-Ninth and King Drive, there is statute of a Black man standing on a stack of worn-out shoes, which symbolize the many Black people migrating North from the South. Cottage Grove Avenue was the area's main commercial strip, and many Jewish families ran businesses along commercial strips like Thirty-Fifth and Forty-Seventh Street.

> From our oral history, it was widely spread among southerners that jobs were readily available in abundance in the north causing my folk and others to migrate from the south into the North. From a negative viewpoint and in the same year that my mother was born, many southerners settled into the Douglas Grand area and because of increasing racial tension, Chicago has one of the worst riots in their history resulting in much loss of life. Yet from a positive viewpoint, business and professional offices were popping up in the Bronzeville area and 47th street because a center for trade and entertainment.

The Regal Theater was a beautiful theater, as far as I can remember, with a large stage, red velvet drapes, red velvet carpet, red velvet seats, and grand chandeliers. The lobby of the theater was enormous, and there was a broad staircase leading up to the balcony. Outside, a brilliantly lit marquee advertised pictures of coming attractions. The Regal closed in 1968 and was torn down in 1971; it should have had landmark status. There was so much history wrapped in that theater. Adjacent to the Regal was the legendary five-and-dime department store, and above that was the famous Madam C. J. Walker Beauty School, where I used to run through playing when we went there to buy peanuts and candy corn mix at the five-and-dime. Madam C. J. Walker was the first Black female millionaire.

The Metropolitan Theater, which catered more to movies and Saturday matinees of twenty-five cartoons and the Three Stooges, was just across the street in the 4600 block of South Park Way, now Dr. Martin Luther King Drive.

The 1960s saw housing units constructed, like the Robert Taylor Homes along State Street and Federal Street, which was just across the street from the high school I attended, Jean-Baptiste-Point du Sable High School. According to history, Du Sable was a Black man known as the founder of Chicago and the first settler. The housing projects lined State Street. In the late 1950s to early 1960s, some of the housing restrictions placed on African Americans in Chicago were lifted, and many families left Bronzeville and moved farther south out of Bronzeville. The result of this for example, from 1950 to 1990, the combined population of Bronzeville and Grand Boulevard neighborhoods declined as people began moving out; the economic base of the area was all but gone. Many of the factories and stores closed. People I knew moved out because they felt they could do better in a better neighborhood. Some of these properties were owned by the residents and were abandoned, not understanding the power of ownership.

There were several historical landmarks throughout the area, some of which I climbed on and played around on, not knowing what they meant. There were Black-owned banks.

The Monument to the Great Northern Migration is the name of the fifteen-foot statue on King Drive/Grand Boulevard (at the intersection of Twenty-Fifth and King Drive). A statue of a Black man standing on top a pile of worn-out shoe soles; he faces north to indicate the direction of his journey. The statue commemorates the Blacks who left the South to come to Chicago to work.

The Walk of Fame has a number of plaques that name people who have lived in Bronzeville. The plaques are cast in bronze and line both sides of King Drive, I played hopscotch, jumping over and around them.

The Quinn Chapel (Thirty-First and King Drive) was built in 1847 and was an Underground Railroad safe house.

Bronzeville had already begun its transition into change and was on the decline when I was born in the mid-1940s. I was growing up there in the late 1940s through the late 1960s and 1970s. It was losing businesses and residents. It was on a downward spiral partly because its residents were no longer confined to that area. The civil rights movement was making it possible to get better housing in better neighborhoods.

I played on and around these monuments and passed by them almost every day of my life. I didn't care about the history behind the plaques and statutes or why they were there. Most of the people

I grew up with and the adults who lived there had no idea of the rich history of the neighborhood, the landmarks, and the treasures they were witnessing. If I had noticed or been told, I might have taken more pride in the community at the time.

Life was hard there. People were poor. At that time, the main foci of life were food, paying the rent, and survival. We were a community and people who respected one another. There were rules to live by, and people raised their children to be respectful. People attended church and wanted their children to be good, God-fearing people. They were good people in a fast-paced environment; they were first generations from the rural South, caught up in something they knew nothing about. Let's take a walk through the decades leading up to the migration.

My mother, Jean, was a sharecropper's daughter, the granddaughter and great-granddaughter of women who were slaves. She grew up with and knew very well that they would not approve of alcohol, smoking, and drugs, and she never used any of it. She and her siblings sharecropped in the fields that were once plantation land, owned by slaveholders. They all picked cotton in the South, harvested peanuts, and chopped sugarcane to sell; they raised their own farm animals, planted their own vegetables, and cured their own meat to feed themselves and their children.

By the 1940s, people were tired of the Jim Crow South and ready for a change. My mother, so I was told, was the most difficult of all the children. She broke the rules, was impulsive and defiant. She was bored of the South and, therefore, was the first in her family to leave home.

By the time my mother was seventeen, she left home on her own, moving to Hattiesburg, Mississippi, and married an army serviceman. His nickname was Red, and they had a child together, who was stillborn. They named the child Willie. Later, Red was killed in an accident, and my mother received a substantial amount of money as a result of his death. My mother's first cousin filled some missing pieces to the story. Before I was born, my mother met my father's mother. It wasn't until later that my mother met her son. He was, at that time, in the army, serving in World War II. My grandmother had a conversation with her son, about a woman (my mother) who lived across the street. She told him that my mother had inherited a lump sum of money and told him to introduce himself to her while he was on leave.

I don't know if it was the truth, but my father and mother got married and migrated to Chicago along with my father's mother, my grandmother, in the early 1940s during the Great Migration of Blacks from the South to the North. This may explain why my mother and my father stayed together such a short period. They divorced some three or four years after I was born.

The Situation of the Women of Bronzeville

I don't believe for one minute that the women of Bronzeville really knew what they were getting into. I am speaking of these women that decided to get into a life of crime. I don't believe they were able to make an informed decision or think things through, but desperate situations required desperate measures, and so they did desperate, irrational things. Perhaps their logic was "Maybe we'd do it for a little while, just to make enough money to feed our children, pay the rent, and put a little away for a rainy day." However, they didn't plan how they would get out; they were somewhat naive about this new lifestyle. When you act out of desperation, you don't think things through. They saw their action as the only option; they didn't see the big picture. The women of Bronzeville didn't know enough about what they were getting into, and they would become the Queens of the Jungle—they had no safety nets to fall back on. They were working territories that had long been the domain of organized crime.

It wasn't just one block where all the action took place. Forty-Seventh and Calumet was the block where more business was conducted than any other block in Bronzeville. The women had the merchandise for sale that many people sought, and that made them the targets of the police as well as the stickup men, drug users, gangsters, and whoever else that didn't like the idea of them taking away business, profits, and customers. But what organized crime didn't realize was that these women were tough, strong, Southern, field-working, sharecropping, house-dress-apron-wearing, pistol-packing mamas! They had nerves of steel—and they were desperate and not easily intimidated; together they were a force to be reckoned.

The dangers women experienced in Bronzeville were very real. Like everyone else, the women knew there were dangerous people (real gangsters, as in Mafia) who lived and hung out in the neighborhood. If you know anything about Chicago's history, you can imagine who these real gangsters were. They were powerful people, and some of them held prominent, powerful positions in society. The Aldermen, for example, were very powerful men and women, but under them were the precinct captains, who had almost as much power. They were responsible for getting out the vote and knowing everyone in the neighborhood. The Aldermen and the precinct captains had the power of getting people elected or not elected—people as high up as mayors and presidents. But you can bet that organized crime had a lot to do with it too.

The people who lived in Bronzeville were making money committing crimes, but not everyone who lived there was dangerous. Those that were living the fabulous ghetto lifestyle were, for the most part, just trying to survive and feed their children. Others were living pretty well—as well as you could in the ghetto. Like one woman— she was from the islands and spoke with a Geechee accent, and she was so little about four feet five inches tall. She wasn't one of the women of Bronzeville, but she was selling heroin and didn't care about anything or what anyone said. Her motto was "If they buyin', then I am sellin'." She did more time than they all did combined over a period of years. She lived the fabulous ghetto lifestyle. Bronzeville was a haven for drugs, drug dealers, and addicts; sometimes they beat the dealers or shortchange them from their merchandise. Sometimes, people would rip off the money or the drugs; sometimes, they'd run off with both, knowing what could happen to them.

The powerful people were lawyers who defended the drug suppliers, as well as the judges and policemen who took bribes and fixed cases for them.

Still, most of the addicts would do anything for a fix. The hardcore junkies were the most dangerous ones. Other junkies, though, were very vulnerable because they were addicts and prostitutes, but they also had principles. They had a sort of "honor among thieves." They would look out for one another and help one another. Drug addicts were living in bondage, trapped because of their heroin addiction and cocaine addiction. They had a monkey on their backs, the hardest thing in the world to kick was heroin. The only way to beat that habit was to never use it, something I learned at a very young age.

Cocaine was a rich man's drug, a white man's drug of choice. Black folks couldn't afford cocaine. Heroin, on the other hand, was cheap, as little as a dollar a capsule. There were people from all cultures and all walks of life who came into Bronzeville. Addiction includes the high they got from the adrenaline rush of ducking and dodging the police or getting away with stealing to feed the habit and the high. I believe the adrenaline rush was more addictive than the actual drug was because, after they got away and fed their habit, they all sat around and laughed and discussed how they got away with what they did. Many went to Bronzeville to buy and sell drugs, sex, or other merchandise, things very small to very large.

Meet a Few Women of Bronzeville

Because my mother, Jean, was a sharecropper's daughter, the grand-daughter and great-granddaughter of women who were slaves, she grew up with and knew very well that they would not approve of alcohol use, smoking, or drug use. She never used any of it.

They and she were churchgoing and God-fearing people; this would be a great shock to them.

By the 1940s, people were ready for a change. They were tired of the segregated South. My mother was bored of the South and of the Jim Crow laws, which influenced her decision to leave home with four of her siblings to follow her.

My mother met my father's mother first. It wasn't until later that my mother met her son, my father. He was, at that time, in the army, serving in World War II. My grandmother had a conversation with her son about a woman (my mother) who lived across the street.

She told him that my mother had inherited a lump sum of money and told him to introduce himself to her while he was on leave. My grandmother Lois wanted him to get to know my mother.

I don't know if that is the truth or not, but my father and my mother got married and migrated to Chicago along with my grand-mother Lois in the early 1940s during the Great Migration of Blacks from the South to the North. This may explain why my mother and my father stayed together such a short period. They divorced some three of four years after I was born, and she moved back to Mississippi for a while and returned to Chicago a few years later.

The other women of Bronzeville migrated during the same period and, as fate would have it, settled in the community of Bronzeville at the same time. Their meeting would change the lives of many.

There were powerful people in the community of Bronzeville strong enough to not use the drugs they sold. The big-time dealers came around, delivered large amounts of dope, and collected their money. They were the ones who made the big money, getting rich off the ghetto and living in the suburbs. They owned the liquor stores and advertised large signs of liquor advertisements and cigarettes, which kept people addicted. They were ready to kill to protect themselves and their drug interests—from the stickup man or those who would try to rob the women, to the police who wanted bribes, to the Mafia, who wanted control.

The one question that had eaten at me for as long as I could remember was if anyone else in our group felt the way I did or if I was the only one having a difficult time coming to terms with and understanding the way we lived and grew up in Bronzeville.

I was very much surprised at the answers given to me by the people I grew up with about our past. They all said the same thing: that they didn't mind it at all.

It was almost like they were wearing a badge of honor the way they spoke about it. For me it was hell talking about it especially during a period when we were living in segregation and poverty. Talking about some things was not so bad when we talked about Jew Town and our mothers taking us there to get Jew Town polish sausage on Sundays and to the flea markets. Jew Town was along Maxwell Street, near where the old Illinois Central Railroad used to be. Black people traveled to and from the south on the Illinois Central train during the Great Migration, and the train had a colored car for Blacks and a colored bathroom and water fountain in the station. Everybody who came west in the north passed through Maxwell Street. Italians, Greeks, Bohemians, Russians, and Germans stopped here for a while; there was no color barrier in Jew Town. Everyone could go there to sell their goods, used tires, old shoes, clothes, etc.

Bronzeville was where many Blacks came; it was sometimes the first stop on the way farther north, like to New York and other places. We talked about race in America, the idea that it was about the color of your skin, even in your own neighborhood. If you were high yellow, you were accepted and treated better than the darker-skinned person in the neighborhood was. It was just how it was another one of those "posttraumatic slave syndromes."

Many people who came to the North from the South during the first migration of the late 1900s were well-to-do Blacks. The Jazz Era treated the large cities well. This was totally unlike the migration that would take place in the thirties and forties. That time would bring a population from the rural areas of the South, all the way from the Mississippi Delta, who brought with them the Delta blues. Most people lived in a rooming house on Forty-Sixth Place and Vincennes Avenue, called the Big House. It was a gray-stone, three-story mansion, once owned by the very rich and elite. Now it was a rooming house; many poor people and people migrating from the South lived there. They rented a room and shared the bathrooms and the kitchen. The Big House was not far from the historical Fellowship Baptist Church, led by the well-known evangelist Reverend Clay Evans. That, of course, was just around the corner from the historical Regal Theater.

Some people got jobs making and selling moonshine. They sold moonshine to make money to feed their children, and some worked at the stockyards and the slaughterhouse there. Our parents lived just a few blocks away from the Big House on Forty-Seventh and Calumet Avenue, on the other side of what was called Grand Boulevard in the late 1880s, when the rich and elite rode their carriages up and down the Grand Boulevard scenic route. A second name change gave us South Parkway, and a third change seemed to finally settle on Dr. Martin Luther King Drive. Forty-Seventh and Calumet was the street where all the happening was going on: the prostitution, bars, drug dealing. You could find everything right there on Calumet and up and down Forty-Seventh Street. The prostitution in Bronzeville was due to the cultural atmosphere there and the live entertainment. There were bars, restaurants, the Regal Theater, the Metropolitan

Theatre—a lot of money flowed from entertainers, blues artists, jazz artists, writers, and poets. There were also a lot of gangsters in the neighborhood. Some women saw a way to take care of their children by renting out rooms to prostitutes for two dollars a date (or a trick). Every time they wanted to use the room, it cost them two dollars. The prostitutes walked the streets day and night from one end of the block to the other, never leaving the block because there was a stream of men going there looking for prostitutes or looking for drugs especially when there was a stage show at the Regal. The entertainment brought in a lot of that kind of traffic. The line the prostitutes used was "Hey, baby, want a date? Three for me and two for the room."

That was something that seemed so sad to me, that they sold their bodies for so little. I have some idea about how my mother began selling dope. She was introduced to it by another woman she met in Bronzeville she became close with. All I knew was she did it, and she made a lot of money doing it. At one time, she opened and operated a barbecue joint. She took care of us others and in the neighborhood who didn't have what they needed. People were suffering. Children were suffering everybody's children. Everybody did what he or she had to do to survive. There has always been more violence in the Black community because people lived in such poverty and suffering, which seems to breed crime. Everyone was trying to survive.

I don't know what the relationship was between my mother and the other lady who lived in same building, but I know they became good friends after they got to know each other, and they began trusting each other. I know my mother was keeping money for her. That's all I knew. When my mother needed help, she was right there to help. My mother was just twenty-six years old when she migrated to Chicago and when she met her friend, who would lend her money and help her with whatever she needed. That is how it all began.

My daddy was out of the house, and everybody else's daddy was gone too because of welfare. That left our mothers vulnerable and alone to take care of us. Those women were strong bound and determined to do whatever it took to take care of and feed their children. Women were alone because that was the only way they could receive welfare, and that was what caused the men to leave in the first place. Welfare had rules that, if you had a husband, you didn't qualify for welfare, and if you had a TV or a radio, you didn't qualify. The welfare workers were nasty, disrespectful, and mean toward Black women. When they came for a visit, they looked under the beds, in the bathrooms, behind the door, and in the shower to see if there was man hiding in there. They belittled these women and men, but my mother and the other women told the welfare worker where she could go and to get the F out of their house.

These women took care of everybody and everybody's children that they could in and out of the neighborhood. People went all the time to them, and they'd say to them "My children need milk, and they need diapers." The women gave them whatever they needed.

Every one of the girls I grew up with all told me the best thing that ever happened to them in their lives was their mothers and what they sacrificed for them. Their mothers sacrificed their freedom to see to it that they had food, shelter, and clothes. Otherwise, we would have gone hungry, and so many others would not have had food or shelter or clothes, either. They talked about being taught right from wrong, compassion for others, and how to treat people and never to look down on others. It didn't make a difference if they were dope fiends or wine heads; they were still people. They are still your elders, and you will respect them. This is a community; everybody in it is part of this community. We look out for one another.

They all felt that they were lucky that their mothers sacrificed so much for them even if they didn't understand it then. We were taught to stay in a child's place and to be respectful to everyone. They said they were never embarrassed by what their mothers did. They felt they did what they had to do to provide for them.

They felt their mothers made them feel like they wanted to be better in life, better than the world around them, better even than what their mothers had or did. They did know enough to know they didn't want to have to do the things their mother had to do to survive. I know I wasn't happy with my mother's life choices, but I know she wanted me to do better and to be happy. That's not too much of a burden to lay down for your children. My mother preached education, education every day. A lot of my age-group were boosters and thieves; a lot of the junkies in the neighborhood were boosters, and they boosted clothes for us.

Remembering what my mother said took away all my thinking about wanting to do anything wrong because I never wanted to disappoint my family; they had so much hope for my future and so much trust in me. I knew, if my mother had found out that I had done anything wrong, my entire family would have been so disappointed in me and I would have been in soooo much trouble! That may sound difficult to understand, considering everything they did, but we were afraid to do anything that would disappoint them. I never wanted to disappoint my mother, my grandmother, or my aunts and uncles. We did what we were told to do, or we didn't get caught. That was sometimes hard to do. Our mothers made sure we had manners and respect and that we followed the rules and went to church twice a week.

My mother fed, clothed, and housed five children and still had enough to help other families. That's the way we were raised. That is why I have the beliefs I have today. I will always help my brothers and sisters. I will always share whatever I have.

That is what my mother taught me. We were a community! No children were going to go to Family Services; these women took in children and raised them no matter where their families were, in jail on the street or just gone. My mother's friend passed away before they all were to go to the penitentiary. My mother took up the job of mothering her children until she left to go do her time. There is a lifetime between us all. My mother outlived the other women by forty-four years.

Do you think that other people would have understood the way you feel about your mother? Do you think they would understand that we learned a lot about life from those people who were addicts, boosters, dealers, and prostitutes? I got some of my principles from them. I felt like I could trust them more than I could trust most people. They taught me a lot about life because they were loyal to one another. They looked out for one another. If one was sick, they shared with them and hustled to help them. None of the stuff that is going on these days—trying to kill one another over a bag of dope! I never heard of such a thing back in the day. What they did, they did it to themselves and no one else.

I ran into my biggest problem with trust outside the community. People from the street, they will be truthful and real with you. It didn't make a difference they would tell you straight up: if someone saw me walking down the street with a cigarette hanging out of my mouth, I could get it slapped out of my mouth. It didn't matter who it was; it could have been hype (a hypodermic needle or injection, a drug addict) or a prostitute. My mama expected me to be respectful.

I knew smoking, as a kid, was wrong, and I would be too scared to go tell my mother, because I knew I was doing something she wouldn't approve of. I could get a whoopin' or punishment from anyone around me. It was a village raising children, and I was one of the children. It didn't matter who was telling you what to do as long as you followed instruction even if you didn't like it. You didn't talk back or act disrespectful. You had to mind. I wasn't in a race to outdo others or be better than anyone else. I just wanted to do the right thing in the difficult world I lived in.

One simple question I had led to a longer story. I was beginning to process my feelings and my life. I wanted to receive much needed validation. I needed answers.

The question I needed an answer to was how they felt.

I mean, the addicts in a nod, hypodermic needles sticking out of arms, blood in the hallways and in the bathrooms, from the injection points after dribbling down their arms. It started to seem like a normal, everyday occurrence in my life. I was getting sick of it. I didn't want to see it or be a part of it anymore. I think we got used to seeing it and played in and around it, day in and day out. We couldn't go anywhere. We lived in segregation; there was no place to run or hide. Sometimes an addict couldn't hit themselves the way they normally did, so some of the older kids would do it for them because they had burned out nearly all their veins. If they overdosed, they saw how others revived them. They'd shoot them up again, only this time with salt water, or vinegar and water. It would counteract the effects of dope.

They could also put them into a tub of ice water and then walk them until they came around.

They'd take the ice pick and bust up the block of ice and put it in the bathtub. Dangerous, for sure, but it didn't scare them. Scares me to think we really didn't realize what they were doing. I was scared to try anything until my brother overdosed and I had to try to save his life.

I was angry when I went to visit them twenty years later. I had already moved out of state after I healed from the assault. After my mother and the other women were to go jail, the whole crew broke up; everybody moved away. My mother's friend died, and my mother and the other women were there for her children. They made some collard greens, baked a cake, and fried some chicken. My mother and Mrs. Becky went to their place before they went to the penitentiary. By the time my mother's friend died, she had stopped all illegal activity, and she had never done a day in jail.

I will always remember where I came from. It's hard to escape what you've seen and been through. I looked at people walking around with syphilis sores on their bodies and abscesses on their hands and feet, and they looked like they had boxing gloves on their hands. They were so swollen and oozing pus from shooting heroin. That life our mamas made was not the kind of life I wanted to live. I learned some valuable lessons. I experienced some heartbreaking things in my life and was lucky enough to be able to overcome many of them. I think our mothers were great people to take the chances they did to take care of us. The way they helped other people in need may not have been conventional—or even right—but they sacrificed their freedom and their lives for their children. Because of what our mothers did, they each paid the ultimate price; they each lost a child to heroin addiction, but I believe it is never too late to stop and turn things around, and they got a second chance at life. Unfortunately, one of my best friends, the daughter of my mother's friend, and my brother began using at the same time, and they both are gone now. It was so painful to watch my friend and my brother go like that. Not even just one of them, but many. I worry most about the children they left behind. When she passed and their father died the same way, the children were left without a mother or a father. I haven't seen them in many years, but I ask about them all the time. I hear they are doing very well. God provided for those children just as he provided for us. It is so important for me to remember them all. Their lives could have been so different if they had been given a chance, yet if it had not been for them, I might have gone in the same direction. I feel the need to commemorate their lives because I loved them all. I wish I would have been aware enough to speak with them about their lives before they passed, but I know how they suffered. Addiction is something in life humans have not learned; it is almost impossible to conquer. For some of those I lost, they couldn't conquer it. We were sisters in a way; we have shared so much pain and tragedy.

Interview with Sue

Sue was a longtime friend. We grew up together, and we lived in the same building. She is gone now, and we had remained friends throughout the years. Her mother was one of the invisible, invincible women of Bronzeville.

She and I had this discussion at my mother's house when I was visiting for the holidays after my sister's death in 2005. We were taking about what history she was aware of about her family. This interview was spontaneous.

My mother was born in Meyerville, Mississippi. My mother and father married sometime in the 1930s and they left Mississippi in 1941, my mother and father migrated to Chicago, Illinois, where they had four children. They settled in Bronzeville, on Forty-Seventh Street and Calumet Avenue across the street from Mrs. Jean and her friend. After a period of time we moved in the same building they lived in on the first floor. My mother migrated to Chicago following her brother he was very tall and a big man. Their sister came later, as did some of her cousins. I don't believe it was a mistake that our mothers settled in Chicago around the same time and in the same place. Their lives became intertwined by fate and they became the best of friends right off. Nothing is ever by chance—that is my thought.

They were partners from the very beginning, experiencing hardships together, having, then losing, and mourning their children. They served time in the penitentiary together. They were truly sisters in every sense of the word.

My mother was bold and brazen. My mother was a strong woman and took care of herself; she was the granddaughter of slaves. They had so much in common like living Jim Crow in the south; I think that is why they got along so well. My father was a quiet man, my mother was outgoing, clearly the matriarch of our family. I knew my mother was in charge because my father allowed her to be in charge. My mother and father were together until she went to the penitentiary. My father worked all his adult life and most of his childhood in the fields sharecropping until his retirement.

I don't know how or when my mother got involved with selling drugs. The women of Bronzeville had compassion for others and didn't like to watch others suffer. They did something about it.

My mother was hard on me and I thought she was so mean. I was a hand full too. I didn't care about what my mother did. It never really bothered me because we had food on the table and other people had food on the table too because of her. I could never have been ashamed of my mother. I loved her. Even now after my younger brother's death, and my other brother's addiction, I loved my mother more than ever. I don't have any regrets for anything she did. I know she was doing what she had to.

To this day, I do things I learned from her. I was just like her, but I soon learned that it was not what I wanted to do. She didn't want me to do it either. Finally, she bought a duplex and got out of the neighborhood out of Bronzeville, as soon as the housing covenants were lifted. We were one of the first families to leave Bronzeville. One of the other women of Bronzeville was the first to leave. My mother left Bronzeville thinking we could have better living standards, and better living conditions but it didn't mean it was always going to be safe for us. Moving out to other neighborhoods could have been dangerous for us having been just post segregation. After segregation blacks could live almost, anywhere they wanted so my mother moved us, but then white people began move out as black people moved in, they didn't want to live in the same neighborhood with black people.

Moving was a little too late for my mother, she had already caught a case. ["charged with a crime by the police"].

Once we moved and my mother had been indicted. I knew she was going away and I worked on turning my life around before it got too out of control. My mother was then able to pay more attention to me, and she taught us differently from what we had seen in Bronzeville. WOW! I could never have been ashamed of my mother. I know I was rebellious and resentful at times. I even stole drugs from her and sold them for half price in the street to my mother's customers when I was just ten and twelve years old to get extra money to go places and do things like go to the Riverview amusement park on the intersection of Western Ave. and Belmont Ave. Of course, when she found out, she whipped me. I did what I saw her do and I wanted money too. I was smoking weed at eleven and getting into all kinds of trouble. I wanted what I wanted, I was a mischievous and rebellious. I can't explain why but I did not live the things I saw. Like you I saw different in the south. I fought a lot—even with my friends—but we made up after every fight.

I had my own customers my mother didn't know anything about. The merchandise I took from her, I was selling for half price. I was always watching to see where she hid her stash. I don't think she knew when I stole drugs from her stash.

If mama moved her stash, I would just mix up what I had left from last time with milk sugar—the street name of what we call lactose now—and bag it up in some tin foil and sell it on the street. Then I'd use the cash to take all my friends to the Riverview Amusement Park.

My mother found out when the people who'd bought from me, would go back to my mama and expect her to make it right. We would be gone all day, and when we returned, I would get my behind torn up. We all got a "whoopin'." We didn't care, because we never got the chance to do anything anyway but watch junkies shoot up and nod. It was our only chance for us to get away from all chaos and we had fun. It was a chance to forget for a day where we came from.

It was worse when my brother Billy found out. When I tried to sell anything again and he found out what we were doing, he would grab me by the hair and drag me home to my mama. He would be so mad at me. We lived on the first floor of a six flat apartment building and you lived on the third floor. My mama beat my behind good and by the time you got to the third floor I could hear her hollin' "Mama, please, I ain't gone do it no mo'!"

I was always getting into trouble, and my daddy was always sticking up for me. I knew deep down I was doing wrong, but still I didn't know. It was all I saw every day. I was mad about it but I was never ashamed. I knew she was trying to give us some of the things she could never have afforded and to keep food on the table. My mother made sacrifices for us, and she took chances on losing her freedom and her life. My mother wasn't a criminal she was desperate. She

was raised in the church in the South. My mother
and father came north looking for a better life,
but it wasn't to be so great. There were no jobs
and no place to go. My mother and father did the
best they knew how to do. I don't know how my
mother got started, I just know that the three of
them met and worked together. Whatever they
did wasn't only for them. There were babies who
were sick, mothers who had nothing and others
who needed milk and food for their children.
We needed to be fed, too. That is the only thing
they thought about. They could do something
to change life situations in the neighborhood, so
they helped a lot of people they paid for school
for some, and paid for treatment for others. Their
selfless hearts had good intention. They just got
caught up.

We moved out because my mother wanted
out. That was before she caught a case, before we
moved. She didn't know it because the indictment
had not come down yet. The only thing I regretted was that my two brothers became addicted to
heroin. They were young—the youngest died of
a drug-induced aneurism; my middle brother is
still using.

My mother went to jail, did seven years in
a federal penitentiary at Alderson, West Virginia.
When she came home, she never did anything
wrong again. She was out of jail for thirty-seven
years before she passed away of a heart attack.
The irony was that the neighborhood she moved
us to away from the hood was a nice neighborhood. When she got back it was just like the one,
we left in Bronzeville and she was once again
living in poverty. I guess according to God's law

everyone will pay a price for what they do in life. That is a commonsense life's lesson I learned.

I have hereditary heart trouble and have lost one of my legs due to a blood clot. My mother is gone she died of a heart attack at age seventy-one. Who knows what life would have been like had she had not been involved with organized crime? It absolutely took a toll on her and on us. I can only imagine what life would have been like. I suppose it could have been worse if she had not done what she did to feed and clothe us.

My friend is gone now too. She passed away due to a staph infection on June 5, 2005, after being admitted to the hospital for another blood clot. The year 2005 was an especially hard year to get through because my sister passed away that year. On January 12, 2005, her son passed away. On January 26, 2005, my two cousins, my sister-in-law of thirty-five years, and my best friend Sue all passed away that year. We spent time together that year before she passed. This interview was done the last time I saw her. Sue was buried in a cemetery on the south side of Chicago at Sixty-Seventh and Cottage Grove. I always think about her being buried there because that cemetery was closed to Black people when we were growing up. It was segregated and had a six-foot brick wall around it. We tried to climb over that wall many times, boosting each other just to get a look inside there. I guess we were curious to know why Blacks were not allowed in there. Today she is buried there next to her mother, her father, and her brother. How ironic! It took forty years from the time we were children to the time Sue was buried there. I returned to Chicago to attend her funeral, and it was the first time I had ever been inside Oak Wood Cemetery established in 1853. How fitting it is that she is now buried there.

I stayed in touch with Sue and learned that she went on to school, lived a successful life, married, had a daughter, and moved to Arizona until her husband passed away. After the funeral, she returned to Chicago, and shortly thereafter, her mother passed away. She stayed to care for her father until his death. It was a stressful situation for her. She'd come back to Chicago to the same situation she left many years ago—her mother was now living in a run-down, drug-infested neighborhood worse than the one we lived in in Bronzeville.

When her mother and her father left Bronzeville, they thought they were leaving behind all that. It was a nice area to live in, but soon, many more were leaving Bronzeville for the same reason. Segregation was supposed to be a thing of the past, and Blacks could move anywhere they wanted to. But the places they moved to soon had become the same as the place they came from. Whites moved out to get away from integrating even though the laws had changed the mindset of the White people had not changed and the behaviors of the people moving in had not changed. While her mother was in the penitentiary, the new neighborhood became the old neighborhood. Sue was deeply saddened by the situation. It wasn't long before she became ill and was no longer able to work. She lost her leg due to a blood clot and lived in seclusion for a time after her father passed away.

Life wasn't the same for her. She was forced to go on social security and live in a senior high-rise. I would go to Chicago and visit her and take her out, and we would reminisce and talk about our past lives. We would visit my mother on holidays. I took the opportunity during those times to ask them the questions about how they felt about growing up in Bronzeville.

The three of us talked about their feelings very candidly the day we visited my mother during the Christmas holidays in 2005. Another person we grew up with us in Bronzeville was with us. I was very surprised at their answers: that it hadn't bothered them the way it bothered me. I didn't entirely see the past as "forgettable" because I didn't want that life at all. I understood their rationality, and the reality was, if they didn't do what they did, we would have continued to go hungry. But their opinion did nothing to dampen my anger and pain.

It was ironic that she survived everything Bronzeville had to throw at her only to die in the place that should have been able to save her, the hospital. There are no words to express my feelings at that time or now. She was still young and had a lot of life left in her. She didn't have to die; she had outlived so much danger for so many years. The three of us were looking toward many more years together as we grew old together.

How fitting that she was buried in the cemetery that was closed to Blacks yet existed in the heart of the Black community for all those years. It was cemetery whose seven-foot wall that we tried to scale around to see what was so special about it that Blacks could not be allowed in it. And now she was going to be buried there, and Black folks were allowed in legally for her burial. That was the first time in my life that I had ever been inside that cemetery that had been closed to Blacks. I'll bet she is smiling from ear to ear because she tried so hard, so many times to climb that wall, scraping her knees to see on the other side. She finally got in and is buried there now that Black people are allowed in. The strangest thing was, my first visit inside Oakwood Cemetery was so peaceful all I can say is "God bless you, Sue. May you rest in peace." I will always miss you! Sue was sixty years old.

Sue's Brother Billy about His Mother, Interview 3

Sue's brother Billy and I have kept in touch over the years, especially since his sister's death. He's been like a brother to me. I lost my brother, and I have been like a sister to him; he, too, lost his sister. We had never spoken about our experiences in Bronzeville until after his sister's death. It had never occurred to me that I had never asked a male whom we grew up with about their feelings growing up in Bronzeville. I guess in part it was because most all the males we grew up with are gone. This has been the future of Black males for a long time—to die young especially in our community.

Since slavery, Black males have not lived very long lives, due to the murder rate or police-involved deaths, dying of poor health conditions or drug abuse. Billy and I check in with each other quite often, and as we were talking on one occasion, I decided to ask him about his feeling. How did he feel about how we grew up, about what our mother did? This was important because we had to work through all of it together. There were just a few of us left, and we needed I needed to know what he was thinking. I needed to know if he felt that we were fortunate that we made it this far in life. We lived through so much adversity and the amazing odds against us—and lastly, how we'd beaten the odds.

I was never more surprised to hear what he had to say! His view was different from the views of the female perspective. His point of view was more similar to mine. I was stunned, and I felt validated at the same time.

Billy was older than us, so he was always a little out of our age range. He hung out with the older kids on the block. I only saw him with just a few friends, but most of the time, we didn't see him at all. He escaped from the madness whenever he could. I have no idea where he went or what he did, and he wasn't saying, but we knew he had a girlfriend outside the neighborhood, and I guess that is where he spent most of his time. He married his wife when they were young, and they are still married to this day.

Billy stayed to himself most of the time. I always thought he was just mean because he would grab his sister by her hair and drag her home if she were about to get into trouble. He was always hollering at her and us, and he seemed so antisocial. It wasn't a word I would have used back then to describe him; I just thought he was mean.

Billy was very handsome and tall, a sweet mix of his parents, who were very good-looking people. The girls in the neighborhood would swoon over him. Billy would not engage with any of us, even though we lived in the same building. It never dawned on me that he knew what Sue was doing, what we were doing. He never said anything until he and I talked about it fifty years later in the context of discussing his sister.

Here is what he had to say.

> You all thought I didn't know what Sue was doing? I did. That is why I was always on her!
>
> I always made her go home and told mama on her, I didn't care if she got in trouble or got whoopins. I was trying to help her to save her because she was my sister and I loved her, but she was fast and determined to get into trouble. I was trying to protect her and keep her out of trouble. I realized the dangers of where we lived and the danger you all put yourselves in. I was trying to keep anything from happening to her. I knew she was bold and wasn't afraid of anything. In fact,

some of the things she did you was afraid to do and afraid for her.

I never thought Billy had any feelings one way or the other about the way we grew up. I was so angry with my own issues, I never thought about the male perspective except when it came to my brother and losing him. I was as afraid for him as Billy was for Sue.

It never dawned on me that he may have had any emotions around how we grew up. In the '40s and '50s, men were supposed to be strong and not think. Feeling and thinking was for women—especially among Black men. I asked the simplest question of him, "How do feel about what our mothers did?"

He replied in such a serious tone—like he'd been waiting for someone to ask that question and to give him a chance to get it all off his chest. His remarks came gushing out like a pipe that had burst.

I really stayed to myself, except for a few friends" but my mother taught me well while I was growing up on 47th Street, the best lessons that I could have ever learned. She taught me by example that I did not want to live the kind of life she'd chosen to live and she taught it to me by example even if she didn't realize it at the time. That is the way I looked at it. The drug addicts, dope dealers, and prostitutes taught me well. What I saw made me wonder how anyone using dope thought they could tell me anything. They were not in their right minds even so how could they possibly think they could entice me to use or sell drugs? Their weakness made me sick. People were constantly trying to entice me to use or sell drugs. All I wanted to do was knock 'em out. To me, they were dead inside; they had no capacity to think for themselves. I would have to be as stupid as they were to fall for that trap. I'd wind up just like them. That's what made me even madder that they could think that I could look at them dying and turn around and say give me some too I want to die like you.

That wasn't me! I could think for myself. The nerve of them to continue to approach me only made me more and more angry. I was angry enough to want to punch their lights out. I spent a lot of time trying to get away. I was trying get away from them telling them to stay away from me and my sister. I did some things to stay afloat in the neighborhood, things I never wanted to do—but there was no place else to go. I left the neighborhood entirely, and after a while, they stopped bothering me. They finally realized how serious I was. I still had to hang out with the guys in my age group in the neighborhood, but I learned to excuse myself when they were using. I was afraid that given enough time they would eventually wear me down.

I was angry about it all the time and all I wanted to do was to get out. I was tired of living like this, tired of being approached and enticed to do something. I didn't want to do the old cliché where misery loves company. That's exactly what it was about. They wanted to see me the way they saw themselves. God forbid I'd get out and make a life for myself! They wanted me down in the gutter with them—they thought that that was where I belonged too.

I got out, but you never forget that pressure of living in that type of life. It leaves scars and to watch my brothers who were not as strong as I was, to watch their lives slip away from them was horrifying. I cannot forget, but I will continue to live my life the best I can.

I remember the horror of watching them shoot up every day in the halls outside the door where we lived. I'd see them in the bathroom, sitting on the toilet shooting up and overdosing. You don't always have to die when you overdose but someone needs to be there to save you! A lot of them overdosed right out of jail and didn't have sense enough to know they should not do it again. They just kept doing it, even though they should have been wondering if their bodies could tolerate the strength of the drug after being clean for a while. I asked myself, "What is wrong with them?" If they survived an overdose, it was because someone was watching over them. I could never do that—putting my life in someone else's hands. Besides [he added sheepishly], I feared needles.

I could never block out my family, no matter what they did, no matter the consequences we had to live with as children, watching the suffering and the feeling of shame, guilt and helplessness. At the same time, our young minds tried to make sense of it all. The shame and guilt kept us down because you don't want others to know where you came from or what you'd done or what your family had done. You feel guilty for many reasons even though it was never about something you'd done specifically. It was a miasma of guilt, almost a culture of guilt, and you spend a lifetime trying to climb out of that hole. Some of us never made it out of that steep dark hole.

You live wondering if the whole thing ever ends. You wonder if maybe someday the drugs and prostitution will not be a part of our families, knowing full well that it's not just going to happen. We will have to work hard at seeing to it that the bad is weeded out because weeds kill. The losses and heartache, the scars it leaves behind will be with all of us forever. We will live with it for the rest of our lives.

Strange to say but I sometimes feel guilty for surviving. I'm glad it wasn't me, but it sometimes brings about overwhelming shame and sense guilt just for feeling that way. It seems to me as if everyone should understand that when adults make decisions, there will be situation that they put their children in. The environment we grew up in had to be justified in some way. Justifying the reasons, reasoning that it may be justified—does not make it right. We are living with the fallout even to this day.

Billy talked about his anger, but all he would say was that his mother taught him well. Like the rest of us, he would never say anything against his mother. He loved his mother, but I could hear in his voice that he had as many issues and reservations about all of it, just as I did.

I found it strange that none of the girls I grew up with felt the way I or he did, or they just would not admit it. Truth be told, I never expected him to respond at all, but I was glad he did. In a way, he validated my struggles. When I spoke to him, the things he said and the things his wife said really surprised me. She was concerned about him because she had never known that he struggled with this. His wife had never heard him talk about his childhood like that. She was just as surprised as I was.

I asked Billy why he was so mean to Sue, and he said this:

> I wasn't mean to her. Y'all thought I didn't know what y'all were doing. I knew Sue was stealing drugs and I knew she was bagging up milk sugar and selling it to people on the street. Thing is, they were going back to mama and telling on her

so mama could make it right. Sue was putting me and mama and everybody else in danger. I know everything y'all were doing that's why I was on her so much because she was headed for trouble and about to fall into that trap. So was y'all, but I could only do something about my own sister. I wasn't mean to her. I was angry, like you, about the activities going on around us and angry at her for being so bad. All I was doing was looking out for her; looking out for my sister. I couldn't help what she was seeing every day and I couldn't stop what my mother was doing, but I could do all I could do to save my sister and wish I could have saved my brothers, fortunately she turned out OK.

After that conversation, I understood him a little better. Now that I know he was struggling to survive like me, I feel less alone, less isolated—less judgmental. Billy has had the same job since he was a teenager. He's been married to the same woman for forty-something years. They have raised their children away from the type of life we were exposed to and raised in. Billy has a brother who is still out there.

I find it difficult to understand that how no matter what you do to change your life for the better, it may take generations to separate your family from its darker past.

I know my own family has been trying for the last two generations to rid our lives of drugs and alcohol. I admire Billy because like my brothers he is one of a few men from Bronzeville who made wise decisions and had the resilience enough to survive the neighborhood and the memories. I wish my brother Jeffro, my sister, Chico, friends, other family, Ty, and all the others might have had that kind of resilience to survive everything that was thrown at them. To this day, both of us are still affected emotionally by our experiences in Bronzeville.

Interview #3 My mother's recollection of being pulled in

The first place we lived was at 4835 Calumet in the basement we lived there when me and your father separated. Not long after that, we moved across the street to 4832 Calumet for a short time. Right in the room next to us was the policy wheel where they drew the numbers for people who had bet with the bookies. In my opinion, the numbers game was a perfect model for what we know today as the lottery. After that we moved to 4749 Calumet. That's when I met my friend. She lived on the second floor and we moved in on the third floor up over her. She was doing well, she was making a lot of money and she was taking care of her family, she was taking care of the whole neighborhood. When we met, we became friends right away I didn't have nothin'. I asked her to help me out and she did. She helped me with you all, buying food and givin' y'all clothes and shoes. In return, I was doing hair, pressin' and curlin' hair for her and her family and the neighborhood. I made two dollars a head. One day, she asked me to hold her money for her. I didn't know why, and I didn't ask why. I was already borrowing money from her and it wasn't enough for me to keep borrowing money from her to make ends meet. I was tired of begging and tired of seeing y'all in hand-me-downs. I hated seein' you teased about wearing other children's last year's clothes and playing with other children's last year's Christmas toys. But I couldn't do no better. Welfare didn't pay the bills, they said I didn't qualify and there were no jobs to be had. I was keeping the money for her and she started paying me and that helped me out a lot. She didn't like keeping her money in the house in case something happened. No one knew nothing about me and didn't suspect anything.

> Later on, she say she needed help, she can't keep taking care of everybody by herself. She say she got five children to take care of, she told me to come on, she was gone teach me how to make some money. I said, "I ain't never done nothin' like this before."
>
> She said, "We doin' this for everybody. We gone take care of the women and children and take care of them that can't take care of themselves. We're gonna send them to treatment if they wont to go, but they gone use this stuff anyway. They was using this stuff when we got here and wasn't nobody tryin' to help nobody. They all is makin' money and ain't putting none back. They ain't helpin' nobody.
>
> "We can help them and send them to treatment when they wont to go, but ain't nothing gone help them if they don't wont no help." I was so green. I didn't know nothin'!
>
> We sent a lot of them to treatment. Some stayed clean and some didn't. We put that money to some good use. We spent a lot a money paying for treatment and taking care of other people's children while they was in treatment and in the meantime, y'all had what you needed.

I did not want to interrupt by saying I never wanted any of it, so I just didn't say anything. I didn't ask for this! She continued, saying she had the hoe house she rented out two rooms for two dollars per date each. It was called a trick, and people then paid two dollars for the room and three dollars to the prostitute for sex. I can hear them now walking the block, saying, "Hey, baby, want a date? Three for me and two for the room." Imagine selling your body all day and all night for three dollars a trick to feed a heroin habit.

People made and sold moonshine for many years to make money to feed their children and others in the neighborhood. These women were special, good, and kind women. They demanded and commanded respect. They never refused anyone anything; if they had it to give, they gave it. They always had high expectations and always put children first, and they put them in their place if they got out of pocket. You couldn't be disrespectful in their presence. They were quiet and soft-spoken, wouldn't say much but would get their belts after you in a minute. They didn't take no stuff off anybody. They didn't drink or smoke or do drugs. It was all about business, survival, and taking care of her children and helping whom they could.

My mother continued, "I was green and desperate to feed my children. I had just come up from the South and didn't know nothin' and didn't know many people. She showed me what to do, how to mix it, bag it up, and sell it. We did good for a time, raised some of the children in the neighborhood whose parents didn't have time for them. We fed them too, sent some of them to college and sent a lot of them to treatment. We fed and clothed a lot of people."

It wasn't long before our other friend moved into the building. She had three children to feed at the time, and she joined in with us. We all joined to try to make life easier for all of us. There was a market for drugs, what with all the people coming into the neighborhood from all over the world! There were rhythm and blues artists, jazz artists, poets, and writers. People came from all over to see them perform at the historic Regal Theater and at the landmark Jerry's Palm Tavern, Teresa's Blues Bar at Forty-Eighth and Indiana, where Muddy Waters performed regularly. Bobby Blues Band and B. B. King performed at Teresa's Lounge and Blues Bar while on break from performing at the Regal Theater. I sat outside with my friends and listened to their music for years until I was old enough to go in and participate myself. I grew up on the Chicago blues in Teresa's blues bar. A small room enough to seat maybe fifty people with a small area to set up a set of drums and three of four other instruments, it was like a juke joint in the South.

My mother commented, "We sold a many a bag a dope, ten bags for ten dollars, or a dollar a capsule. After a while, selling an eighth of an ounce for thirty dollars to whoever came to town to perform was commonplace. That was a lot of money back then! After that, the police at Forty-Eighth Street Station right off Wabash and downtown at Eleventh Street station on State Street, they were being paid taking bribes to look the other way, to tell us when a raid was coming down, and soon, moneymaking was little because they was all in on the take and getting paid too. After a while, there was no money to be made paying the police for protection."

That is as far as my mother would go except to say how dangerous the people were. Organized crime was all around us. I don't know if they all had those kinds of ties; if they did, they wouldn't have discussed it. I could fill in the rest of what went on with my family. Long after one of them passed away and the other moved away, my mother and her remained connected and were still in the game until they went to the federal penitentiary at Alderson, West Virginia. They became partners with two other women in the neighborhood—two sisters who lived a couple of blocks away—and the four of them became a force to be reckoned with. All four of them went to the penitentiary together and shared the same cottage. They had to be careful of what they said and did because there had been several gangland killings in Bronzeville in November of 1963.

I met the people who were murdered gangland style and knew they were dangerous, not that I was afraid of them. I wasn't. I was much more afraid for what my mother's involvement with them would mean. I sometimes wonder if she was afraid or if she realized the kind of people she had gotten involved with.

Another Friend Who
Lived in the Building

She is gone too, and I did not get the chance to interview her before she passed away.

She, I, and Sue were raised in the same building. Her mother was one of the first women to move to Bronzeville. We were the same age; the three of us were friends as far back as I can remember.

We went to the same schools, had the same friends, and hung out together. The three of us lived in the same building. Of course, like all sisters, we fought all the time for one reason or another, but we always made up before the day was done.

I was the poorest of the three, and I always got their hand-me-downs and their last year's Christmas toys. They always teased me about wearing their last year's clothes and playing with their last year's Christmas toys. That was one of the things we fought about! Every year, that was what I got for Christmas: their last year's stuff. I would always run home crying, and my mother would push me back out the door and say "You never run away from any fight! The only way to stop the fighting is to let them know you are not afraid." I didn't like to fight; I was afraid. I didn't like the scratches in my face; they hurt too bad. Besides that, I blacked out with no knowledge of what took place.

The fighting did eventually stop, and we became very protective of one another, but they would always find something different about me to tease me about. One of those things was they felt

I was too sensitive for them. They were the ones who thought it was funny to watch prostitutes turn tricks, peeping through the keyhole or watching over the transit, standing on milk crates. I hated that! If they were doing something wrong, I would leave them until they were done. I would not participate. I didn't want to disappoint my family. Besides, I had the Ten Commandments ingrained in my head, the "Thou shalt not" verses, and peeping at prostitutes was not one of those verses. I felt so guilty and so sorry for the way the prostitutes were treated. Not only was I teased for not participating; I was teased about having green eyes and called high yellow because of my skin complexion.

She and Sue teased me about that for a very long time as kids and later even as an adult. The three of us became great friends. We hung out together even after they moved away. We would find ourselves walking miles to meet up with one another. We'd go to sock hops and school dances and social center at school every other Friday night. As I think back, we were about fourteen or fifteen years old in 1959 when Dick Clark's *American Bandstand* came to Chicago, the first and only time, to the State and Lake Theater in downtown Chicago. We were there, but the fact is that, until *American Bandstand* went to Los Angeles, Black teenagers never appeared on the show.

All three of us went with a boyfriend; I went with Clem, and me and Clem won the dance contest that day. Our prize was an album; we were so proud being on television. Three teenage Black girls from the Chicago's Bronzeville appearing on Dick Clark's *American Bandstand*! That was one of our most memorable experiences. We were so proud of ourselves, and Clem and I winning a dance contest on *American Bandstand* was the best. It was the first time ever in Chicago, and they allowed us three Black couples for the first time to be there.

The last I heard, Clem had died of an aneurysm in the 1990s. We did a lot of things together, like go to the Peps a dance hall for teens every Wednesday and Saturday night. After the Peps was over at 5:00 a.m., we would walk through Washington Park and sit at the lagoon, watch the sun rise while listening to Sid McCoy's jazz show. His signature sign-off at the end of his show was "Hey, hey, old bean and you too, baby." Then he would play Frank Sinatra's "In the wee small hours of the morning, when the whole wide world is fast asleep." We also listened to Yvonne Daniels's show, *Daniels' Den*, another legendary jazz program in Chicago. Sometimes we went to Bud Land, where the legendary Herb Kent, the cool gent, was the DJ. He had a radio program for over sixty years in Chicago. It was not until the drug use began that we drifted apart. I continued to look for my friend and my brother to make sure they were all right. I helped them when I could. She and I were like sisters until the day she died five days after her forty-sixth birthday. I had just gone to see her and to wish her a happy birthday. Remembering them and the impact they had on my life is part of the reason I am writing this book and maybe in part the reason I survived to tell their stories.

It's important to me that I can remember the ones I loved in a way that they will never be forgotten and, at the same time, be an inspiration to someone else.

We used to hang out at Andersons' playground on the next block late in the evening before dinnertime. Everyone had to be home before the streetlights came on or else. We played on the swings and the merry-go-round with the boys. Sometimes we played "boy chase a girl, catch a girl, kiss a girl." When the boy caught the girl, she would have to kiss him. It was innocent fun, but I was never the girl anyone wanted to catch. I might have been too timid, or maybe I wasn't cute enough or sexual enough. I guess that is one of the reasons I didn't get pregnant at an early age. I never indicated I would be easy, and I am glad I was not the one they wanted even though I was as pretty. During the daytime, we hung out at the playground, playing jacks or baseball and, sometimes, basketball with the boys. In the winter, we could ice-skate there too or play games inside the field house.

Momma and Me

The early years

In the early years of my life, I was very close to my mother. That was a time when my mother, my grandmother, and my father were all together; I was a happy little girl. We had rules and structure, and there was nothing to be afraid of anymore, not like it was in the South, when the KKK roamed the countryside, placing fear in everyone. We had to attend church every Sunday. We lived by a schedule and a routine, and we attended school every day. We had extended family in the South that we visited often. We were poor, but we were happy we knew of our very proud family heritage. Life then seemed so very simple.

Our lives changed dramatically in the wink of an eye; things became different when my mother and my father divorced. I was about four years old, and we moved one block north of where my grandmother lived in Bronzeville.

There were no trees at the new place, no grass, only abandoned cars, vacant lots where you could see and hear the L train running all day and night. There were drugs, drug dealers, prostitutes, pimps, hustlers, and gamblers on the street all day and all night.

How could we have lived one block away with no prostitution, no drugs, no pimps, and we had grass and an orange tree in my grandmother's backyard? How could it have been so different?

This was the beginning of my anxiety.

The story for us as children was what we experienced in our lives before Forty-Seventh Street and Calumet Avenue in Bronzeville. While I can't argue that we did have some good experiences, it was the horrible ones we ultimately carried through our lives. When we visited our extended family in the South, we saw trees and grass and wide-open spaces in the country, which we never forgot.

Returning from our visits, we went from the Rural South—to a neighborhood on South Side of Chicago, where the smell of whisky and wine, stale beer, and pee was inside and outside every building on the block. It was horrible. Inside the apartment wasn't much different as we lived in a kitchenette apartment in the front two rooms and shared the kitchen and the bathroom with other families. The junkies got high in the bathroom and left their spikes on the sink and their drug paraphernalia out in the open for all to see. Sometimes we would go to use the bathroom, and they would be there nodding, sitting on the toilet seat, blood dripping from their arms.

Kitchenette apartment, Chicago

It was more than I could comprehend as a child. I knew life was going to be bad when I first saw Forty-Seventh Street and Calumet Avenue. I somehow knew that we would have to learn to make the best of it in order to survive. I knew my mother was doing the best she could. Being newly divorced and alone with five children in an unfamiliar place was hard. We were living in a segregated society, and we knew it was going to be even more difficult after my father and grandmother were no longer in the house together. It was a sure sign that things would get worse.

My grandmother and father were just up the street, and while my father paid child support—twenty dollars a week for me and my brother—it certainly was not enough to feed all of us. My grandmother helped as much as she could.

My maternal grandmother sent care packages at Christmastime. They were the highlight of our holiday season. My grandmother and great-grandmother sent quilts they'd quilted themselves to ensure we had covers to keep us warm during the long, cold Chicago winter nights. They sent what the family sharecropped for a living: raw peanuts, sugarcane, and coconuts. We would bake the peanuts in the oven and would have the whole building smelling good like peanuts. People would be coming up to our door, wanting to know what it was that smell so good and begging for some. My grandmother also sent a shoebox full of her homemade, special coconut cake, which we all called Granny's Cake. She'd made it with egg white icing and stewed apple filling.

She fried chicken and shipped it through the mail, wrapped in wax paper and dry ice placed in a shoebox tied up with string. It was always chicken because it kept better than other meats did. Sometimes it was all we got besides the fruit my paternal grandmother sent us. The apartment smelled like fruit like oranges, which sometimes took away the other smells that permeated throughout the building and the neighborhood.

The strangest gift I remember my grandmother sending was a shoebox of red clay dirt. It was to ward off iron deficiency. We would eat it like children ate candy; it was tradition in the family. I can tell you that I couldn't eat it now, but it was traditional back then! She'd send us stalks of sugarcane that we would peel, chewing on the stringy pulp, squeezing the sweet juice out of it with our teeth, and then spitting the pulp after we'd sucked the last trace of sweetness from it. Granny sent coconuts too, and we would take the hammer and pound a nail through the top to put a hole in it. Then we could pour the coconut milk out and drink the cool sweetness. Splitting the empty shell open with the hammer, we scraped the sweet meat off and ate it. Sometimes it was the only thing we got for Christmas and the only sweet treat we got.

When we went to our paternal grandmother's house, she always had lots of fruit during the holidays, and the house would always smell like Christmas. Her house was always festive and full of joy during the holidays even though she only had two rooms a kitchen and a bedroom. The smell of fruit, jelly cakes, and sweet potato pies permeated the two-room small basement apartment. Sometimes, when she was baking, she would allow me to stir or mix the cakes. She would tell me what to put in the bowls and let me mix the cakes. This is how she taught me how to cook, just like my grandmother in the South did when we visited for family reunions. My maternal grandmother put all the girls to work in the kitchen, preparing food for all the family members. When we lived with my grandmother in Chicago; we roasted marshmallows and hot dogs in the backyard over an open pit she built of bricks and stove racks.

More important than anything is that we always had three meals a day no matter what! When we moved out of my grandmother's house, we were lucky if we had any meals a day. My mother would tell us she was tired of us going hungry, going with holes in our shoes, and wearing hand-me-downs. She promised that one day, she would do better, that it wouldn't be like this forever. We fought over cardboard in the neighborhood because we used it to cover the holes in our shoes. We'd trace our feet and cut out the pattern and place it in our shoes to keep our feet from touching the ground. There was so much broken glass all over the place from wine bottles and beer bottles, so we needed something to help protect our feet. We didn't have coats, hats, scarves, gloves, socks, or shoes. If we had a coat, it didn't have buttons on it, and our shoes were usually too small or too large and had holes in the soles. We did not have enough to buy a ten-cent roll of toilet paper. We used paper bags and newspaper.

The Struggle

We lived in segregated Chicago. There were no jobs anywhere. Women in the neighborhood received $125 a month in welfare for five children if they were lucky enough to qualify—but only when there were no men in the house. That meant that, if you had a husband, you had to get rid of him when the welfare workers came around. Fathers would leap through windows, drop down emergency ladders and up the stairwells to the roof or next door. The welfare system forced the men out of the house.

This forced the neighborhood to become a de facto matriarchal community of women raising and taking care of children without husbands. The welfare workers would come to visit then search for men hiding in closets, under beds, and behind bathroom doors to make sure that only women and children lived in the place alone. There could also be no radios, televisions, or telephones. They would disqualify you because—they were told—that anyone who could afford a phone, a TV, or a radio wouldn't need help feeding or clothing their children.

Everyone was on the lookout for the welfare worker so that we could tell our fathers and mothers when the government workers were in the neighborhood. In the book *Black Mother Goose*, a book of Black nursery rhymes by Elizabeth Murphy Oliver, one of the rhymes reads, "Daddy, daddy get up and out; the welfare worker's about."

Daddy would get up and go out the back door or out of the window like other fathers in the neighborhood did. They would go to another house or down the street somewhere to outwit the welfare worker. It was this behavior in the neighborhood that led daddies to have babies by other women. The fathers soon got tired of being humiliated like that, and finally, they left for good.

Remembering the Abusive Treatment of Women

I watched as my uncle beat my aunt. My mother, though, always fought back. She would not sit by and take it, and that set the example for me. Whatever happened to my mother when she was growing up set the tone for how she wanted to be treated, I do not know.

I saw women beaten up daily from one end of the block to the other, and everyone acted like it was normal. The women themselves thought it was normal because the men who beat them said they loved them after they beat them. I could not understand that concept of love, and my mother underscored that when she told me never to allow any man to treat me like that. Even without her wisdom, I had it already made up in my mind that it was not going to ever happen to me.

No man would ever put his hands on me and get away with it!

Resentment and Search for Understanding

For a long time, I resented my mother for not being able to provide for us. I resented my father for leaving.

Although I resented my mother for the decisions she made to start a life of crime and I understood her rationale, it still really bothered me to this day. I would rather have been poor and in the South, living in segregation and seeing the Klan in their hoods, terrifying the countryside and dealing with racism, rather than live like how we lived in Bronzeville. At least those in the South knew where they stood and knew how to cope with racial issues. Racism was out in the open there; people willingly admitted to being racist.

In the North, racism was covert, hidden by the patina of the "abolitionist north defeating the slave-owning South." The truth was that the North was just as racist, but the undercurrent was harder to fight. It was very hard trying to come to terms with the undercurrent of race in the north. The pretense to not be racist but, all the time, stabbing you in the back, it is still that way to this day in the workplace, in schools, in housing, and in economics. I think I have been harassed and experienced more racism by White women and Black men in the workplace. I would rather speak my mind get fired or just leave a job than to take it. I see a lot of women who will put up with it to get a head to get what they want only to come out years later and cry foul. I think most Black women wouldn't take it. This is just my opinion: we have too much pride and will put them in their place even if we lose a job. My mother was that way. She had a lot of pride; she wouldn't take it, unlike this so-called Me Too movement, going along with the program to get what you want and later crying foul. Or like the woman who had sex with a president, saving the semen-stained dress and giving it to her mother for safekeeping until she was ready to expose him, and they call her a victim when she set it up. If I had done that, my mother would have knocked me out of the door backward. The first thing was, I would have never taken something like that to my mother, out of respect, and the second would be that I would have never been following a man on his tours and making advances, especially to a president. Her intent was obvious. It was a setup, and unfortunately, he fell right into it. In my opinion, she was no victim, and she is still exploiting this to this day, especially for money. She has no morals or dignity.

I knew what my mother did was for us, and the other women of Bronzeville did what they thought they had to do for their children to survive, but what was done was never discussed. It was like no one had feelings about it; at the least you didn't ever talk about it out of fear. The children never talked about it because we were not allowed to talk about it back then. It was the age of "Children are to be seen and not heard." It was normal, everyday life, and we didn't get to voice our opinions. Once we were adults, we never spoke about it though we had experienced so much despair, seen so much death and destruction, and suffered under Northern racism. I was determined to ask my mother to share her thoughts about her life in the North, her life of crime, and her life after the penitentiary. It was long after then that I decided to ask her about it; she was eighty-five years old at that time. I had to talk with her; it was now or never. I asked her how she felt about her life and being involved in crime. I didn't think for a moment she would ever answer, but she looked at me in that mama-looking way, the way she looked at you when she forbade you to continue as though you had really done or said something wrong; That "Don't ever ask me that again" look. She hesitated as though she were in deep thought for a long time, and then she began to speak. When my mother finally spoke, she said, "Way back in the 1940s, we had just come up to Chicago from Mississippi and moved to Bronzeville, a place that was well-known, where anybody who was anybody came to when they traveled north. That's where many people come to from all parts of the South in the '30s, '40s, and the '50s during the Great Migration from the South." She said, to my surprise, "We sold a many bag of dope," and she stopped there and didn't say any more. Finally, she felt comfortable enough to tell the whole story.

The Bronzeville Neighborhood

The neighborhood of Bronzeville was a historical place. People came from all over and spoke different languages, dialects, and spoke with different accents. Some spoke Geechee, some spoke Gullah, some spoke Creole. Still others spoke with a Southern dialect. People from Mississippi had an accent different from that of people from Arkansas, people from Louisiana had an accent different from that of people from Alabama, who had an accent different from that of people from Mississippi and Arkansas and in other surrounding states. There were doctors, lawyers, nurses, musicians, entertainers, comedians, poets, and writers who visited, lived, and worked in Bronzeville.

There was a market for that Southern soul food; you could find every kind of ethnic foods sold in Bronzeville: the best soul food, the best barbecue, chicken shacks, frozen custard stands, Pearl's Place, the Queen of the Sea, for more than six decades; Gladys soul food, more than six decades; Lane's BBQ, more than ten decades; Latin foods, and Asian foods like Chan's pan-fried chicken. The best pan-fried chicken in the world and just about everything in between could be found in Bronzeville. Lane's on Forty-Seventh and Prairie, serving in the basement, was a stopping point for every entertainer who came to Bronzeville. Lane's had pictures of every entertainer that ever came to Bronzeville to perform or write on his wall that they had been visiting his place—and he had been there for more seventy years and was 113 years old when he passed away.

There was a lot of money to be made in the food industry. Bronzeville was a great place, and author Nathan Thompson called it

"America's Black downtown" in his book, *The Policy Kings*. Organized crime in Bronzeville ran a numbers game known as the Policy Wheel, which was declared illegal, but the federal government made it legal. It was a sort of lottery, perhaps was even *the* model used for the future state lottery. The policy wheel was run in the apartment next to ours. They used the same cage back then as the lottery does to draw numbers out of; the only difference was they pulled numbers written paper rather than the balls they use today. The numbers under wrote many businesses in the neighborhood until it was deemed illegal, and now it is legal.

There was plenty of illegal gambling in the city. Poor people played the numbers, trying to win enough money to make ends meet. It wasn't much—but it was a chance. In addition to gambling, the joints were havens for pimps, hustlers, and drug dealers. As a child, I supposed it was not all bad, we children had our share of fun and our share misery that drew us all very close. We played children's games, played hopscotch, jumped double dutch, and played made-up games together, like root the peg. We didn't have a lot to do, no computers or games or cell phones. We had to use our imagination, and that made us very close because we had to interact with one another. Late in the evening, the boys doo-wopped on the corners, singing and harmonizing while the girls sat and listened.

My mother never verbally apologized for what she put us through. Even so, we knew she loved us with all her heart and soul. She just never knew how to express it, busy trying to make ends meet. The truth was that most of the people in the neighborhood didn't know how to show affection. You just had an abiding faith that the love was there.

Once we were grown and gone, my mother spent the rest of her life trying to make up for everything we suffered through. There was a lot of irony to go around, but worst of all was the price she and her accomplices paid. Was it all worth it? In a sense, we all paid before it was all over with.

Punishment for the Crime

Their punishment was, all but one of them, to be sent to the penitentiary, everyone except for the one with whom it all began—she died of a heart attack on Christmas night 1964.

The woman left carried a lot of stress for a lot of years of being born and raised in the South with Jim Crow, to being raided by the police and forever looking over their shoulders in the North.

Growing up, looking into the faces of these women and seeing the pain they suffered after losing their children, I felt that it was sometimes almost more than I could bear. Certainly, I was suffering the pain of losing my friends and my siblings, but I was blaming my mother and her friends at the same time. They all lost a child to drugs.

As the others went away to the penitentiary, they looked out for one another—that's what people did. Her daughter was a lifesaver for us. She helped to provide for us while my mother was gone. Sometimes I would wonder where we were going to get money to eat, and she always came through for us.

As difficult as it may be to understand and put into perspective—the fact that we were also taking responsibilities and the jobs of our mothers, who'd gone to prison for drug dealing—it was a normal thing to do in a wildly abnormal situation.

My mother's friend, Mrs. Jackie, was a lifesaver. She sent food to us all the time when we didn't have any. I think that, for her, the stress of her life as a child and losing her mother took a toll on her life. She died very young at fifty-two years old. I loved her very much for all she did for us and everyone else. If it had not been for her encouragement, faith, and confidence in me, I don't know what would have happened while my mother was gone.

Reflecting on when my mother migrated to Chicago and to where I was born, in Cook County Hospital, was a critical time in our lives; it was the beginning of it all.

After I was born, my mother returned to Mississippi. I was just two years old. She said times were so hard in Chicago. There were no jobs, and people were living on top of one another. She said segregation was worse in the North than it was in the South and that we lived in a "concrete jungle" void of trees and grass, fenced in by tall concrete buildings. The streets and alleys were made of cobblestone and the place where streetcars ran by rail into and out of Bronzeville.

My mother didn't like living in the South, but at least she knew where she stood. In the South, racism was overt, but you knew it and could get along with it. In the North, you didn't really know where you stood, but that wasn't enough to make her stay in the South. She eventually moved back to Chicago after my brother Jeffro was born.

My mother's parents remained in the South; her father died shortly after she returned to Chicago in 1950. Three of her siblings, a brother and two sisters, followed. Two of them migrated to Milwaukee, my mother and her sister came to Chicago, and a sister migrated to Minnesota. My uncle, who went to Milwaukee, had a family tale about his flight from Mississippi, with the Ku Klux Klan on his heels. He'd done work on the voter registration drive with a well-known civil rights leader. My uncle was threatened with his life and had to leave. My mother and a sister sneaked him out of Mississippi in the dead of night to safety, like many had done for slaves so many years before. He was never the same again.

When we reached Chicago, it was just my brother and I, until my older half sister and half brother by my father's first wife came to live with us. After that, my mother and my father got a basement apartment across the street from my grandmother. We continued to spend most of our time with my grandmother, but that didn't last too long. My mother and my father soon got a divorce. Soon after that, we moved a block farther north of where my grandmother lived to Forty-Seventh Street.

As Chicago was segregated, Bronzeville was one of the only places where Blacks could live and work in the city due to the housing restriction. There was one biracial family in the neighborhood, who lived upstairs on the third floor. I couldn't understand it, especially why they lived in the building and we lived in the basement. I wondered if it was because the mom was White. It never occurred to me they may have lived there before us—which they had—but then, I was only six.

The mother was White and very well received in Bronzeville; the father was Black. They had three children, two boys and a girl. It was very uncommon for White people to live in the Black neighborhood during this period. I had never heard of white people living in a black neighborhood. I did not know very much about race relations, but I knew that it was uncommon for a white family to live in a black community. I believed—the way a child does—that, if you had Black children, you were Black and, you had to live with in the Black neighborhood, but I guess it wasn't the other way around.

I did learn some forty years later that the mother wasn't white but biracial, and she had a story to tell. Her daughter wrote a book that explained that her mother *chose* not to pass for White as she could have. The author's mother's sister chose to pass for White; with that estrangement, they lived apart and did not speak for many years. I recognized the mother and the daughter on *The Oprah Winfrey Show*, telling their story, but I had no way of reaching out to them. I so wanted to speak with them, but we had lost contact many years before when we moved. It was so nice learning their true story, and it cleared up a lot of questions for me that I had as a child growing up.

I had an older half sister, my father's daughter by his first marriage. She was raised by my grandmother. She and I never really got along because from my point of view; she thought she was so grand and so much better than I was. My father and my grandmother favored her over the rest of us because she had the lightest skin color out of all of us—she was what was called high yellow, a term for Blacks who also have quite a bit of White ancestry. The term was in common use when I was growing up, but you don't hear it very often today because it is often considered offensive. I always thought my half sister was White. Anyone who was very light skinned was White to me. There was always conflict in the Black community over light and dark skin. My grandmother had straight long auburn hair with very light skin. My sister was tall and thin, with auburn hair and light brown eyes, and I had hazel eyes like my father's hazel eyes. My grandfather's eyes were like mine, light blue or green or gray hazel (depends on the light).

There were lots of issues in the Black community surrounding skin color in those days. You were less noticeable if you had darker skin, and people paid more attention to you if you had lighter skin. This was inbred from slavery and still exists in the Black community. I guess some thought I was lucky—I had hazel eyes, so some thought I was high yellow too, but most of my attention came from my eye color.

This was both good and bad. In the neighborhood, I was treated in a very negative way by my friends. They called me little white girl and teased me because they thought I thought I was better than them.

Mind you, I didn't think that way, but because of my heritage from my father's side and my mother's side of the family, I had to fight a lot, and I got beaten up because of it. As much as it pains me to say so, my grandmother picked her favorites as well. It was obvious to me that she favored the lighter-skinned children in the family. I knew she loved us all—but she treated us differently based on our skin color—and it was something she was brought up with from childhood. As I'm now an adult reflecting on it, it may be that her feelings were directly related to the behavior and the treatment of slaves.

The master deliberately pitted their slaves against one another; the lighter skinned worked in the big house, and the darker skinned worked in the fields, thinking they were better than the others. This was all a part of the master plan, the divide-and-conquer methodology. Most of the girls I grew up with preferred the light-skinned boys with the so-called good hair as I did until I grew up and understood the dynamics behind the way we thought. It was a learned behavior. There was clearly a color issue within the Black community that made us feel inferior to one another, depending on the shade of color you were, which determined how you were treated. Some of my siblings were treated according to the color of their skin. The lighter skin color you had, the better treatment you received. I was so aware of it and felt guilty about it, knowing there was nothing I could do about it. This complicated my existence even more—a community that was all Black and had the same prejudices within it that the world had of us outside it. It is and was the behavior taught to us that filled us with hatred and prejudice toward one another.

Mending Led to Communication

I had tried for many years to mend my relationship with my mother.

Once I had mended some fences with my mother, I asked my mother to talk to me about her life. We had grown closer in later years, and I felt confident enough to believe that I had earned the right to ask her about her life. I had also learned how to accept her for who she was. As part of my own healing, I had forgiven her for what she did. She was, after all, my mother.

I had so many questions I wanted to ask her. But when I told her I wanted to write about all this, she wouldn't hear of it. She just looked at me and wouldn't say a word, staring at me in the way that only she could out of the corner of her eye. Ever since I was a child, those looks made me want to shut up and forget the whole thing. It was as if she were silently saying, "You know better, girl! Don't come here with that mess!"

Once I explained to her what it meant to me for her to discuss this with me, she said, "Honey, I ain't proud of the life I lived and what I did, but I did what I had to do to survive." She'd shook that index finger at me and pointed at me, just as she had when I was a child and she was being firm in saying what she meant and meaning what she was saying. She'd shake that finger to confirm that you understood her. But this time, she kept talking, "I am proud of my children's success. All that I did and all that happened in spite of me and what I had done, look at all of you now. You know I always wanted the best for all of you. You turned out the way I wanted with morals and common sense."

That was the first time she ever talked about any of her life of crime with me, and she did so with a tone of regret. It was a tone she'd have never taken in the past, and she assured me emphatically that it would never happen again. She was reluctant to say, but she did, to my surprise. I, on the other hand, at that time, was in a different place in my life than I had been in earlier years. I told her that I had forgiven her, but I had not forgotten all that had happened to her and to us. I wanted to say something, in particular, something about not all of us surviving. I let her know that I clearly remembered losing my brother, my sister, and my friends. I was not trying to make her feel guilty. I know what she would say, "Honey, they was weak." She could not stand weakness.

I told her that it was important to me to talk about these things for me to be able to understand why I had such an enormously hard time trying to find myself and my place in life. I wanted to understand so that I could have some idea of how to raise my own children to become good citizens and to put an end to the reign of crime, drugs, and alcohol abuse in our family. I needed to figure out why my children were so much affected by the way I was raised and how my own upbringing could affect my children and even my grandchildren. I needed her to know—and I needed to hear for myself—that destruction is what drugs and alcohol abuse do. They ruin families for generations and destroy lives. I just wanted an end to this infectious disease in our family. Even though she never used drugs or smoked cigarettes or drank, it still ran rampant through our family.

I was worried that my own actions would affect my children in the way my mother's actions affected me. I wanted to know how to stop the trend of marijuana use, cocaine, and heroin and alcohol abuse in our family and get it all out of our lives.

My mother and I discussed forgiveness, and I told her that I understood why she did what she did. I was there, and after many years, not only did I know why she did what she did, but I also understood that she'd done it because we were hungry, had no clothes or shoes to wear; it was obvious why she got involved.

As a child, I went to school many days hungry and, in the winter, wearing a coat with no buttons, no hat, no scarf, no boots or socks, and having holes in my shoes. The Windy City's winters were long and brutally cold. We walked a mile to school and back in that kind of weather. I knew that, once she was involved with it all, it was hard for her to get out. I think she finally understood that I understood her motivation even though I was still angry about it.

For the first time ever, she began to talk about her life. Every other time we'd tried to approach the subject, she'd say, "A child should stay in a child's place and stay out of grown folks' business."

This time, she said a few words at first, and they were to warn me not to write about her life and the people she was involved with. She was clearly concerned that they were powerful people and they would kill me or have me killed if I talked about them in a book. I was not concerned because so many years had gone by and they were all gone. My mother was eighty-five years old at the time this conversation took place, and she was the only one still living of the women of Bronzeville and the major players in organized crime.

Others with whom she was involved were still alive, like her attorney, who eventually became a supreme court judge in Illinois. He was indicted on charges of racketeering, conspiracy, extortion, and obstructing justice in the eighties during the time I was questioning her. Even before she was indicted and convicted, she must have known that he was someone she should have feared. He was suspected of having Mafia connections because every one of the men murdered gangland style in the 1960s streak of murders had connections to him. He was convicted of his crimes and did twelve years in the penitentiary, and he died just a few years before my mother did.

I didn't leave Chicago until after my mother came home from the penitentiary in 1971, and I was now twenty-five and just as angry as when she left us.

I had stayed home taking care of my siblings as long as my mother was gone. I was still a teenager myself when she left; people tried to split us up, but I would not have it. We wanted to stay together. Once again, I was parenting my mother's children. My grandmother had gotten sick and could no longer help us out. We all pulled together. My youngest brothers worked for the Cedar Federal

Government Jobs program after school. My other brother, JR, went to work at sixteen and worked the same job for forty-four years!

My two younger brothers worked their way through high school on the Cedar Program and then went on to college and worked their way through college. My younger sisters contributed what they could, and one of them left Chicago and got a job in Washington, DC.

The two others were too young to work. This is the saddest part—my thirteen-year-old sister got pregnant, and another brother was using heroin at a young age. All this was because of the environment we lived in. It had long-lasting effects on us and our family. Heroin, prostitution, robbery—these were all easy ways out at that time, and the consequences for that were just too harsh.

When I was thirty-five, I left my hometown of Chicago after I was done with the surgeries on my face. That was fourteen years after my mother had come home and told me there wasn't room for two women in her house and I had to leave. I was six months pregnant with my first child at the time. It hurt me terribly because I had nowhere to go, but I left anyway.

I was too proud to let her win me over or put me last again. I felt that no one could understand that kind of hurt. I had taken care of her children for years while she was gone! As a child—a child!—I had taken care of *her* children when I was seven years old. I'd hustled pop bottles and beer bottles to feed the five of us all under me, and she did that to me!

I turned away and walked on the street and spent the next two weeks hustling pool day and night, hanging out in the gambling joints all night and hustling pool in the daytime until I won enough money to get a what we called a kitchenette apartment—it had a tiny sink with running water boxed in with cabinets, a bathroom I shared with others, and a living room with a window that looked over the street. It was all I needed a place to lay my head.

By the grace of God, I was able to keep moving forward. I was good at gambling, and I was one of the best woman pool shooters around at a time when there were no women pool shooters I knew of, and I could beat the boys. I was doing okay. I could afford my own place, and I was six months pregnant; that hardly slowed me down.

After my son was born, I started a temp job working at the University of Illinois in the accounting department and soon was hired in a permanent position where I worked and went to school for the next fifteen years.

Then out of the blue, my mother left the kids again and moved in with her longtime boyfriend, who had money and property.

Of course, I was angry with her, but there was nothing about choice involved. She had an opportunity to start over, and she took it. At twenty-six, I moved back in with my brothers and sisters and their father to help him in the projects. My younger sister got pregnant a second time. She was fifteen when she had him, and then she gave him to the father's family.

The matriarch of that family died, and they sent the baby back to stay with us at two years old. My sister wasn't very connected to him, so his raising fell on me. By this time, I was twenty-eight, my own son was three, and I was still living at home, taking care of my siblings. That was when I was assaulted in my bed while I was asleep, and that was when I knew I had to leave Chicago.

Jeffro, Edward Louis, and Me

My brothers, the only two I had then, were different shades.

Jeffro was my complexion, and Edward Louis, my father's son by his first marriage, was considerably darker. I believed he was treated worst of all, but both of them were impulsive and mischievous and stayed in trouble all the time. Like the character in Richard Wright's *Black Boy*, they were very rebellious.

I read the book many times, and it reminded me not only of my brothers' lives but also my own life. There could have been a book called *Black Girl* too, but Wright's book depicted the lives of young black girls as well. It showed the poverty, the oppression, and the racism of the Deep South, where he grew up, and the Northern version of all of them when he was a young adult.

Jeffro was kind of sad as a boy. He didn't smile much, especially as we were being raised during segregation. Jeffro couldn't understand why he was treated differently by society, and he couldn't get his life to go the way he wanted it to. He despised the way Whites looked at him. Knowing there was nothing he could do about it made him angrier still. He would always ask questions about racism. He wanted to know why things were the way they were for Black people in the South and in the North.

He and I were very close, and I remember my mother telling him what he could or couldn't do when he was in the presence of White people. He hated that there was a protocol for how to act when in the presence of White people. There was another protocol for behavior around the police if you were a Black male. He was reminded of it every day. It was a drill for Black boys and common for Black parents to educate their children—especially the boys—on what to say, how to act, and what not to say and do in the presence of the police. Say the wrong thing, and maybe get killed. There was card on the NAACP website that could be printed off and carried in your pocket to remind you of what to say or what not to say.

We were all taught to be quiet, say "Yes, sir" and "No, sir," never to talk back, and never to run. If you ran, they would shoot you in the back just because you were Black. Sixty years later, and it is still the same, Black boys being shot in the back.

Can you imagine having to train your children to be afraid of the law enforcers, who were supposed to be there to protect and serve? That was in the fifties and sixties. Forty years later, I find myself teaching my own children the same protocol.

My brother was very confused and hurt the most by this, and that translated into anger. How do you expect a child—or anyone, for that matter—to understand that others hate you only because of your skin color? You had to be taught to fear the world because there is so much hatred for you because of the color of your skin.

My brothers were troubled young men, and the rate at which Black men were dying in urban areas was climbing at a terrifying rate just as they are today. The irony of his life is that he died young as a lot of Black young men died at the hands of the police at that time. He was shot in the back six times by Chicago police on April 2, 1981, at thirty-three years of age.

So many factors played a role in his life and murder. I refuse to allow him to be just another statistic. Segregation, racism, and poverty played profound roles in his life as they did in the lives of many others and mine and in his death.

I loved my brother with all my heart. He was my protector. No one could bother me, and no one was ever good enough for me in his eyes. He would make me so sick sometimes, he would tell every boy or every man, "Stay away from my sister, man. You ain't good enough for her." Boys were afraid to talk to me.

Jeffro was short for a man—five feet seven inches tall. He had a twenty-five-inch waist in pants, a size-eight-and-a-half shoe, but he walked tall; he could hold his own. Jeffro and I hung out together. We had the same friends, did the same things, frequented the same places. We were best friends even though he was ten months younger than I was. He acted as though he was the older one, and I just sometimes went along with it because he was my brother. Mild mannered, he loved Elvis Presley, Liberace, and Sammy Davis Jr. When Jeffro was a little boy, he'd imitate all three of them. It was uncommon that he, a little Black boy, would choose Elvis and Liberace to idolize. They were both White males. Why not other Black male performers? Maybe he was fascinated by Liberace's bling—though this was long before bling became popular and the word was used.

Sammy Davis Jr., I could understand. He was Black and one of few Black role models of the time. Jeffro taught me how to shoot pool, shoot dice, and pitch pennies to the line for money. He was good at all of them, and I was just as good as he was. Sometimes he couldn't stand it, and he'd get so mad when I'd beat him out of his money. We were teenagers then, and when our mother was out doing her own thing, he and I was out hustling pop bottles and beer bottles to turn in to the grocery store for the deposit to buy food for us and our siblings. We would keep a few pennies to gamble with to make money for the next day's meal or our evening meal. Sometimes, after Jeffro turned twelve, my mother would take him to the gambling joint with her.

My mother loved to gamble. She would gamble all day and all night, sometimes leaving us to take care of ourselves or me to take care of her children. I was angry with her for taking him with her. I knew she was introducing him to more than just gambling. I couldn't understand why she couldn't see what she was doing. I was thirteen at that time, and I could see it. Most of the people who were gambling with her were high rollers, dope dealers, pimps, and hustlers.

I didn't want that for my brother. I knew he was vulnerable and would fall right into the trap because he was already angry, maybe even manic-depressive. The fast lane was the last place he needed to be, all he needed to send him in the wrong direction.

My brothers wouldn't go to school. My mama would take them to school through the front door, and both of them would duck out of the back door. They were ten and twelve. They ran away from home often. They were defiant; I could understand why they lived with the hate. It was all about the color of their skin. They had to learn to protect the neighbor and were expected to protect their sisters while getting beaten up on the way to school in racial incidents. We had to walk a mile every day to school and through a White neighborhood; we were accosted on several occasions and had to fight to get to school. If we didn't go to school, the truant officer would come to our house and sometimes take us away. We had to walk through the valley and face the gangs called the Valley Boys. The valley was close to where President Obama's house is in Hyde Park today. Back then, that area was predominantly White. The boys had the task of keeping the girls safe. That is how the gangs the Disciples and the Vice Lords got started. The young men were told to protect the neighborhood and their sisters and because all of us had to go to church every Sunday. The boys began to call themselves gangs; it was supposed to mean the protection for the community, and the names they gave themselves, Disciples and Vice Lords, came straight out of the Bible. In Bronzeville, after all, at one time or another, there were Italian gangs and other organized gangs throughout the Chicago area.

Not many people know that the names for the Disciples and the Vice Lords were taken right out of the Bible. It was what they learned in church, and they were considering themselves protectors of the land that they lived on in segregation. It was never meant to be what the gangs are today. They protected us. Drugs and prostitution were always a part of Bronzeville because of the entertainment there. When the hustlers, pimps, and drug dealers began to exploit young and the poor, using the children as a means to make money, the war on gangs grew larger and more sophisticated in recruiting techniques and making money. That was a large part of the downfall of Bronzeville.

I hated my mother for her role in the demise of my brother, and I asked her one day why she was taking him to all the gambling joints. She said to me, "Bitch, you just mad because I won't take you."

She often talked to me that way and accused me of messing with her men. She would sometimes put her men before me, before us.

She knew they were hitting on me but blamed me instead. I loved my mother, and I did not tell her when they hit on me because I knew it would hurt her, and I understood the abuses she experienced in her life in the South. I, too, had experienced those from dirty old men, but I was too strong to let them get to me. But sometimes, when they thought I was going to tell her, they would tell her I hit on them. I never wanted to make her sad, because I knew she had a rough life.

That day she said that to me was the day I saw my brother's death flash through my head when I was a teenager. I'd had always had visions of his death coming in his thirties. I saw it because I was born with a gift to see things like that. I just never wanted to acknowledge it until then because I was always afraid of it.

Dreams and Premonitions

It was just like remembering the first memory I had of my life or my existence before I was born. For over forty years, I tried to understand what I thought was a continuing dream. I tried to tell myself it was just a dream, and I dismissed it as a reoccurring dream. I thought it would all go away, but it never did. Those thoughts stayed with me through my every waking hour.

The dream I am talking about is remembering the darkness in my mother's womb. I was too afraid to tell anyone for fear they would think I was crazy, just as I could sense things like danger or death or feel things that were about to happen.

What could this be, and was there a connection between my prebirth experience and my premonitions? Could it be déjà vu, the feeling of having been there before? I am sure some of you have had that feeling before. The feeling that maybe you have been someplace you've never been to before.

I once asked a therapist about what I thought were dreams. I thought it was like being aware of my existence before I was born. She said that it was a prebirth experience. She explained it to me. I didn't know what to call it or how to describe it; I just knew it was my experience, and I was too afraid to tell anyone else about it.

She explained to me that others had the same experience, and it had been studied by professionals. I asked if she thought these experiences had any meaning in my life and my experiences today. She said she didn't know and couldn't explain it. I would have to be the judge of that. I did some research, and I found several personal accounts, all similar to mine, all of them indicating that our experiences meant that maybe there is something before and after this life. I so want to believe that! If there is, then I will see everyone again, my mother, my brother, my sister, my grandmothers, my nephews, and my friends.

At times, I have certain feelings—you can call them premonitions, if you want—but I know that something is going to happen. It is so scary and crazy to know something bad is going to happen before it happens and then to know that there is absolutely nothing you or anyone else can do about it. I had that same feeling of fear the night I was assaulted and perhaps could have done something about it. I could have left!

Five months before my assault, when my brother was murdered, I was listening to a radio program that was incredible, and the subject was about people who had died calling their loved ones to tell them they were all right after they had died. This was important to me because my brother called and spoke to a student worker in my office. I was out on break. When I returned, my student worker informed me that my brother had called and left a message; she said he said he was all right and that his name was Jeffro. I could not believe my ears. I said, "Are you sure that is what he said? That is my brother who was killed." She said, "That is what he said. I would not make that up, I didn't know his name."

It was at least twenty years before I shared that experience with anyone. I finally told my mother. I told her how guilty I felt about not being there, and after all these years, her response was "Honey, it was not meant for you to be there. He was just trying to let you know he was all right, not to scare you to death. It wasn't meant for you to be there." She said it with such conviction as though she knew that these things might have happened in life, and she said, "You don't fight it." she said it as though it had happened to her. My mother was wise like that, and I was relieved that she understood what I had experienced and never questioned the validity of what I had told her without question. It was hard enough working through my feelings of loss and hating myself for not being there when my brother called. I still question if it really happened and why it happened to me. I didn't want these things to happen to me, and I don't really want to know the fate of another.

After my prebirth experience, I don't remember much except being around my grandfather's neck, looking at my mother and her siblings, sharecropping in the fields in Prentiss, Mississippi. They were picking cotton, harvesting peanuts, and chopping sugarcane.

Survival in the 1950s

I worried about my mother a lot all through my life as a child and an adolescent.

From about seven years old, just about the time she began her illegal activity, I worried about her. During that time, she would be gone a lot. I had to take care of her children. We had different fathers, but in our culture, if you have the same mother, there is no such thing as being half brothers and half sisters; you are brothers and sisters. Sometimes my mother would be gone for days. My brother Jeffro and I would hustle pop bottles and beer bottles off the street the next morning after a night of people getting high and drinking. We would take the empty bottles to the store for the deposit and then buy lunch meat, cookies, milk, Kool-Aid, potted meat, and crackers. Lunch meat was ten cents a pound; potted meat, a nickel; milk, a quarter; bread, twelve cents—a dollar went a long way in those days. This would be our breakfast and dinner.

If we were short of cash, as we always were, sometimes the old Jewish man named Irving, who owned the basement store, would extend credit to my mother and the other women of Bronzeville. Our neighborhood had once been an old Jewish ghetto, and after many Jewish people moved out, those who owned businesses there remained.

The man who owned Nate's Shoes on Forty-Seventh Street extended credit to a lot of the women in Bronzeville if they couldn't afford shoes and socks. They were a lifesaver to our families. If it were not for them, sometimes we wouldn't have had shoes on our feet. Before Nate started to help, we used cardboard to trace around our feet, make a cutout, place it at the bottom of our shoes to keep our feet from touching the ground, rocks, and glass. Sometimes we would fight over the cardboard, over who needed it the most.

I had four siblings to take care of at that time. I carried Junior, the youngest, on my hip. He was the baby and just beginning to walk. I tried to keep the other three by my side to keep them safe but ended up chasing them around, trying to keep up with them instead. It wasn't easy. I didn't have my mother's authority. There would be three more to take care of over the years. I was only seven when it all began. I didn't know the details, but I knew that, when she was gone for long periods, she was trying to get money to feed us. My younger sister recalled that she tried to get welfare and remembered a social worker coming to the house and telling our mother she didn't qualify for welfare because she had a TV, and she searched the house to see if there was a man under the bed or hiding in the bathroom or behind the door. My sister said our mother told the social worker to get the F out of her house. Those were common things that happened to women back then, the kinds of things and the type of scrutiny women had to endure from welfare workers. The workers were intent on humiliating black women—it's what they did. Anyone would get tired of being belittled all the time. In the 1950s and early 1960s, welfare reform was limited to various states' attempts to impose residency requirements on welfare recipients. Some called these "man in the house" rules, which cut off benefits when a man lived in the home.

The history of Blacks in America—and even the history of the invisible Black women in Bronzeville and throughout this country—is long, sad, hard, great, and historic.

My slavery history is only two generations from mine. I knew most of my history growing up, I knew my ancestors came from Africa, and I knew their entry point in to the country and what part of Africa they came from. What I did not know was where they came from, what country. Through my research, I learned that I am 41 percent Nigerian, 17 percent European (Irish, Scottish, Welsh, Scandinavian), 11 percent Ivorian/Ghanaian/Congolese/

Cameroonian/Senegalese/Malian. I am also 12 percent American Indian. Migrations from these regions are traced to Mississippi; South Carolina, where my great-great-grandfather came in; and Virginia African Americans.

Where I came from to where I am today is a whole other world.

I am now educated, giving back to society, being a productive citizen, having taught in a college setting, working in a high school with youth, and working toward a PhD. Not bad for a high school dropout, born and raised in poverty and segregation. Most of my siblings are healthy and living productive lives with no drug use. They have struggles here and there, but that is a part of life.

Now if we can get our children to do the same, we will have accomplished something great.

Though this is brighter than it could have been, it is not the end of the story, either, as the trials and tribulations of Black Americans continue every day, every night, every hour, and every moment of every day.

The women of Bronzeville were God-fearing women. On their journey, as it was a part of the Great Migration from the South, and as daughters of sharecroppers and granddaughters of slaves, they were taught to be honest and trusting and God-fearing. They were taught to go to church every Sunday pretty much the same as the migration after the Emancipation Proclamation in the early 1900 of Blacks moving from the South to the North. The question anyone would ask about these women would be what happened to them to make them resort to such drastic measures? What could have possibly possessed them to make them turn to a life of crime? It was a matter of survival for the whole family, and that is the irony of this entire story. We were in danger no matter what. We were in danger of starving, freezing to death; our apartment was always freezing cold, and the landlord would not buy enough coal for heating in a timely manner. We were in danger of the most horrific kind of poverty, and no one should have to live that way. We were in danger no matter what they did to survive. Due to the hunger pains I suffered and the glass in my feet from the holes in my shoes, I would have made some difficult decisions or choices of my own if my children were in the same state. At times, I did have to make some difficult choices when my children and I were without food, shelter, and clothing. Despite that, I found that I had to ask this question: why did I have so much anger and rage inside me if I understood so well why they did what they did?

These women weren't raised like this. They had never encountered anything like what they had ventured into or seen in Bronzeville. They must have been truly desperate! I saw two kinds of women—kind and loving, caring and God-fearing—but at the same time, I saw them as women with nerves of steel who had no fear and would use their pistols without a second thought, making decisions they thought necessary to the survival of their families.

They became responsible for everyone on the block, not because they wanted it that way but because that was what they did. They felt compelled to help everyone who needed help. They did it to help themselves. People began to look to them for help and depend on them. That kind of trust and respect can put people into situations that they are not able to get out of; they didn't want to disappoint those who were depending on them. I think at one point they wished they could take it all back and get out of the game because it became too much of a burden for them to shoulder. They knew it wasn't going to be easy, but they soon discovered that they had to form relationships with gangsters, policemen, addicts, and lawyers. Once they were in, they never anticipated how difficult it would be to get out. They either had to be tough enough to stay in and stay alive to survive it all no matter what the consequences or to die by the sword they'd unwittingly created.

They chose to become as tough as they needed to be to stay alive. It was not the life they had anticipated, but it was the life they now had to live. I think it was a relief for them when they eventually had to go to the penitentiary. Incarceration was their only ticket out. Forcibly removed from it for years, they would return home and would be out of organized crime without incident. It would be up to them to stay out even if they were accosted to get back in. It would be a tough choice, but they could not buy back in. They would have to stay out. But that wouldn't be for many more years.

Right now, they had the respect of everyone in the community because they did not take *shit* and were as ready to pop a cap in anyone's *ass* in a heartbeat. They really had no other options: it was either them or whatever force they were up against at that moment. I don't know all that they did because I did not see everything, but I know that they followed up on any threat they made. They had to or get run over. It was "do or die" to withstand the riffraff.

It was far too late to turn back. It was as though they had a target painted on their backs. There was a lot of loyalty there to them, and people who lived in the community watched their backs; people respected and appreciated what they had done for them and their families. These invisible, invincible women gained a reputation not just in Bronzeville but from Chicago to New York and beyond. People knew where to go to and whom to see when they visited Chicago.

They were tough businesswomen and carried their own weight not only in material goods but also in information. They went to the penitentiary with everyone's secrets. They had a chance to cop out, to cop a plea to have their sentence reduced, but they chose not to take others with them. Their relationship to one another was one of loyalty and respect. I did not understand the way they went about their business without fear and with the respect they had for one another. I thought that it was just the way it was, but I was forced to look at the truth about them. I saw it every day in the way they held on so very tightly to the Bible right next to that gun inside their apron pocket.

They'd read the Bible every day. They walked with Jesus in their apron pockets every day and the equalizer in the other pocket. To me that had to be it because it kept them safe from harm. No matter what happened, they were spared. Going to the penitentiary was part of God's plan. They stayed alive through everything that happened—and that was my greatest fear that something bad was going to happen to them. Bad things did happen, but they were there to talk about it. God kept them alive, and my prayers were answered.

They never appeared to be afraid of anyone in the community. If they were, they never let on. I am sure they had to be afraid of something, but they never showed it. Why was that? I don't have any idea except for the fact that they walked by faith, and they knew, if they showed any weakness, they would be in deeper trouble or maybe even dead.

For example, one day, the stickup men came to rob one of the women, and she stood tall and fierce. She wouldn't let them into the apartment, and she had her pistol in her hand and let them know, if they tried to go any farther, she would blow them away. That happened to the women often, and they'd protected one another because they lived in the same building. They kept lookouts, and if they saw anything suspicious, they warned one another and let everyone know they were there ready to act if need be.

Survival: My Instincts, Apprehension, and Suspicion

I grew up around the same people my mother and the other women of Bronzeville did business with. It goes without saying that I had a lot of apprehension and suspicion. It wasn't fear, just apprehension and suspicion about everyone.

Sometimes, children are more trusting than they should be. I was not. I was more suspicious and cautious than most children my age were. I didn't like what was going on around me. I hated it all, but I was helpless to do anything about it then. I was just a child with no power. I couldn't act, but I could learn, and I did. I learned to live with it. I learned to play the game as well as I could and as well as it could be played to survive. I kept my eyes and ears open. I was an observer and a listener. I listened to everyone's story and vowed that whatever happened to them would never happen to me. I watched the pimps and how they treated women, how they beat them and made them turn tricks and then turn around and be nice to them. I was not going to fall into that trap. I watched the junkies turn out one another and dealers dealing, and I wanted no part of it. I learned a lot by being a listener and watching, I had to learn to survive in this world of madness and chaos.

I can appreciate that I was taught not to trust anyone. I can appreciate that I was taught not to speak to strangers. I can appreciate that I was taught to never allow people to hug me or to sit on anyone's lap and taught never to ask anyone for money or anything from any one—not even a relative. Probably that was one of the things that saved my life and the lives of some of the others who survived the neighborhood. I knew not to defy any of these rules or else.

The only exception was if my mother or grandmother approved of it beforehand. I had good reason not to trust people, but children are sometimes very naive. I didn't want to believe that people could be capable of perpetrating horrible crimes and abuse on others, especially children—even my mother. Despite what my mother and my grandmother said, it was difficult for me to think of people as being bad and untrustworthy. It is just as difficult today for me to understand why people are so mean to one another and to witness the terrible things they do to one another. I have learned how to put people into perspective and to judge them as individuals, but as a child, I had no such skills. This was obvious to me especially after Pinky Lee was abducted. I followed all the rules.

When we were about nine, we were walking to the store, Pinky and I. We were going to buy candy. My grandmother was watching us walk a half a block up the street to the corner store as she always did. Her parting words were, as always, "Remember to look both ways for cars crossing the street, and don't stop to talk to strangers!" Those were always her words when she didn't go with us.

As we crossed the street, we looked both ways. As we approached the store, we saw a man standing on the corner. He spoke to us, and I knew better than to stop and/or to speak back to him. Grandma was watching. She was watching Pinky too, but Pinky didn't follow instructions. She stopped in front of the man and said, "Hey, mister, you got a dime?"

I turned around, and I said, "Grandma is not going to like you stopping. Come on, or you gone get me a whoopin'!" Because I knew my grandma meant what she said and said what she meant.

I didn't stop, but I turned around to see my grandmother running down the street as fast as she could. I did exactly what I knew I was supposed to do: I went into the store. I thought I was going to be in trouble, but I did the right thing.

When I came out, Pinky Lee was gone. My grandmother was screaming "Stop! Stop! But Pinky Lee was gone." Pinky was never found from that day to this one. Her mother suffered so much that she began to drink constantly. I did not see Pinky's mother often after she disappeared. When I did see her, she was almost unrecognizable; she was drinking so much. After two years she was gone—she died. She'd drunk herself to death.

That was lesson enough for me, to not trust anyone and to do what I was told to do. It is a long and lonely life living that way, not trusting anyone, building a wall around yourself so that you didn't get hurt. That is the way I lived for a long time. But I never forgot about Pinky Lee, the seriousness of what could happen. Even living in segregation, if you went too far in any direction out of your neighborhood, the same thing could happen due to segregation.

Fear and Frustration with the Struggle

There are so many women who struggle for equality, who struggle for mere survival. There are many African American women who were and are in the same position as that of the women of Bronzeville even today. They struggle to live and feed their children; they live in poverty, always struggling to make ends meet.

Back then, I was unable to understand why these women were so angry. I thought they were mean and coldhearted. I was not able to understand that the stress and pressure they were under, not being able to make ends meet, not being able to feed their children, had created them. They were firm toward the people they did business with, but I guess they were treating business as business and not taking any chances. They were, after all, doing illegal business with other people who were themselves conducting illegal business as well. If they let their guards down, the price for getting caught was jail, maybe even death. We were taught to live with caution, always mindful, and to keep an eye out for the police and the stickup men.

The women and their children—we had become prisoners in our own homes and in our own community, trapped by the place in which we lived. It was not our home any more than it was the dope house and the heroin shooting gallery. I saw the good that came out of what they were doing, but right alongside it, I saw the bad; there was a strong irony there.

I could have done without both. Call it selfish, if you want. Maybe I say it that way because those who grew up with me felt differently about it than I did. They felt happy about it and fortunate that their mothers loved them enough to see to it we all had proper food and clothes no matter how they got them. I saw it differently. My wildly mixed emotions, deep conflict, and anger at everything around me had no way out. All these did were to build up, and they came out when I got mad enough. I had no idea how to control my rage.

While I admit it took guts for them to do what they did, it took even more guts to know and recognize that they could not get out. They had no choice but to continue in organized crime to feed us. It took guts to stay in when they figured out it wasn't going to be easy to get out. Their very lives could have been taken if they tried to get out. The lives of their children—us—our very being was in danger too. This became something I know weighed heavily on their minds.

Many days, I saw the worry on their faces, and I know when my mother sat with her bible, reading it. She was worried. They worried about the police kicking in the door, being able to pay them off, worried about the stickup men trying to find a way in to rob them, and all of us children being in danger all the time—both inside and outside of the house, worried about being able to pay bills. I don't know which was worse, but they still managed to see to it that we all—including people in the neighborhood—had food to eat, clothing on our backs, and a roof over our heads. They watched one another's back when the hammer was coming down from any danger they were about to encounter. They were tight that way, and no one could come between them. They took everything in stride, faced the music, and kept right on bringing up the kids, helping those poorer than themselves and keeping everyone as safe as they could.

Overcoming the Oppressors and the Police

They had the cops, the stickup men, the dealers, and the Mafia bosses they had to deal with, and the police tried to get them to tell on one another, but they stood strong and firm. They were willing to go down together rather than let outsiders bring them down one by one. When they were locked up for the first time on conspiracy charges, I was shocked that they said they didn't want us to get them out. Instead, they wanted anyone who was going to put up bond money to give it to their children. They may have even been afraid of being killed for fear they would flip; jail was a safe place for them at that time. After my mother was arrested, my mother told me not to worry, that she would be fine, and she had comfort because she knew I would take care of her children. That seemed to be her primary worry at that point. She told me not to allow anyone to separate us no matter what. We needed to stay together.

These women of Bronzeville had gotten so big they became the persons to see for the celebrities coming in to perform at the Regal Theater. In those days, the Regal was a major place for anyone who was anyone. Like its larger cousin in New York, the Regal Theater hosted jazz artists, blues artists, and R & B artists—the biggest names in the business. They needed connections to get their drugs.

Women like my mother and the others were it, but they'd also attracted the attention of the feds—the federal agents—and they were being watched. They'd been targeted for some time. They'd eluded the police for years, and not one of them could catch the women of Bronzeville dirty in over a decade. It was almost like the women were invisible and could slip in and out and around the town. The cops never did catch them dirty.

I remember one time the police tried to raid the house, and they couldn't get in through the bars on the doors, and Blackie barked as loud as he could as he always did.

We lived on the second floor, but a few days later, they got in, and we woke up with guns in our faces. We couldn't figure out how they got in. We thought they had scaled the walls to get in through the windows, but they came in through the garbage chute off the pantry. Even though they thought they were sneaky, they didn't find anything in the house.

That made them angrier than ever. Another time, the bars on the door stopped another raid. No one was home but me and my little nine-year-old sister, who was playing in the hall. They grabbed my sister and put a shotgun to her head to force me to open the door by threatening to shoot her.

That was the first time I laid eyes on a man I will never forget. He would misuse and abuse children to try to send the women of Bronzeville to prison. He was the one who put the shotgun to my sister's head. He was the one who had the police search the children— seven and ten years old—by putting their fingers up our rectum and vagina, searching for drugs.

I disliked that man then, and to this day, I cannot get him out of my head. Though the women of Bronzeville like my mother would eventually go to prison, he had nothing to do with that. As far as I am concerned, he abused me and my sister sexually and violated our innocence by allowing them to search us the way they did. It took a long time to get over that. That's why I do not trust the police and many others have little trust for the police; we all have our personal encounters with them.

The women could have turned the state's evidence on one another. Lord knows the cops tried to get them to, but they refused to do that repeatedly. The cost of giving in would have meant putting their lives and the lives of their children in jeopardy.

If they did get caught with the goods, they chose not to take anyone else with them. They believed that if "you do the crime, you do the time." When they were gone, other women would see to it the children were taken care of. Or so they thought.

I know that my mother did not know the anguish we were going to experience at her absence just as she had not acknowledged the anguish we experienced due to her illegal activities. Nor did she know how long all of it would affect our lives. I believe that is why she did everything she could do to help us when she returned home from prison. She would not let anyone want for anything if she could help it. It was almost as though she were trying to make things right. But it was too late for my brother and sister; it had already cost them their lives.

I'd learned how powerful and dangerous the neighborhood could be. For some reason, I had hope and faith that things could be different someday. Otherwise, without hope, I would not have survived, and without faith, I could not have made it. None of us would have made it. I understood that my mother could not do any better than she was doing under the circumstances. We were locked into a private hell that which we lived in, in Bronzeville. We could not get out because there was no place for us to go. We lived in segregation and due to restrictive housing covenants intended to discourage integrated housing opportunities.

It really didn't mean much that they were making money for a short period. We couldn't move out of the ghetto due to the housing covenants. But what it did mean was that we had food, clothes, and a roof over our heads for a time. The women of Bronzeville shared with those who were unable to help themselves, to keep families from going hungry, and to provide children with milk and diapers. That was the telling thing about them; they had compassion in their hearts for others. At the same time, they were indirectly responsible for the pain and suffering of others.

People in the neighborhood were very grateful to them and respected them because, otherwise, their children would have gone hungry. Some of the children might be dead if it were not for these invisible women.

Even so, it was still a problem for me.

For example, I remember the little boy next door whose mother left him and his siblings alone all the time. One day, the youngest boy was running around with no diaper on. My mother saw him on the porch and made me go see what was going on.

His brothers and sisters showed me that he'd drank a can of lye and was foaming at the mouth. I was screaming for my mother to come and see. She did; she grabbed him and rushed him to the hospital. The lye had eaten up his mouth, but he didn't die. My mother paid the doctors' bill. But in the end, he and his brothers and sisters were removed from their mother. Things like these happened all the time—children falling out of windows and eating stuff they shouldn't, parents leaving their children with others and not coming back to get them because they couldn't take care of them. Our mothers never left us, and they took in those children whose mothers did leave them. It was not always the mother's fault. They were mothers who were just stressed and couldn't handle it; some mothers passed away.

It was all part of the lives of those of us who lived in Bronzeville in poverty.

Living there in poverty was one of things that fed my anger; that made the rage in me burn hotter and hotter.

Against All Odds, Survive!

Back when I was a girl, Forty-Seventh Street was an unusual kind of a place. Everyone was in on the money. Even the pharmacist was making money selling quinine by the jar, which was illegal—but the pharmacist didn't care. A lot of money was involved because everyone used it to mix it in with heroin. Dormin sleeping aid capsules, quinine, milk sugar, and Ritalin were all sold over the counter at that time. Imagine that Ritalin, something prescribed to give to our children for ADD and ADHD, was also something so powerful that junkies shot it into their veins for a high or to keep from getting sick from withdrawals. When Ritalin was sold over the counter legally, junkies used to give us a dime to go to the drugstore to buy it for them. It was legal to sell over the counter until the early 1970s. I think about it now, and I would never have allowed anyone to give it to my children. Other merchants were making money because people were no longer asking for credit; they were buying with cash.

My life was probably in serious danger most of the time just by being a teen and knowing some of the characters in the neighborhood; that alone could have gotten me killed. But even more interesting was how I learned to manipulate situations to play the game to ensure my safety. It was all a game in life, and the prize was about who was going to survive and who was not. It's like the old saying, "the survival of the fittest." If you were weak, you were not going to survive.

I learned that the game never changes. Only the players and the names change; the game stays the same. The beat goes on whether you are there or not there. There is always someone to take your place, and I was determined I was not going to be captured by the game being played in the place I grew up. I was going to do whatever was necessary for me to survive until I could find my way out and to live a different life.

It was important for me to think about more than just surviving. I wanted to give back and help others to understand that they too could have a different life. But first I had to survive. It was too sad that so many didn't understand the rules in Bronzeville. It wasn't that I was young and too naive. I was very much aware of my surroundings, and I was a listener instead of a talker. I wanted to know everything so I could learn how not to get caught up.

I listened to everyone's story. I listened to my parents and grandparents, who often said, "Do as I say, not as I do." I was compassionate about what was done to them and what they experienced during segregation and how they overcame the oppression, prejudice, racist attitudes, and the legacy of slavery.

Everything I saw and heard that was negative in my life made me stay to myself. I was trying to build my confidence and trying to be positive. Everything I heard, I would say to myself, "That ain't gone happen to me." All day every day, I repeated that statement to myself, "That ain't gone happen to me." Every day, I repeated those words to myself, "That ain't gone happen to me." There were tragic, sad stories all around me. I could not see myself in any of those situations for the rest of my life, even though I was already living it. I could not see me being here living like that for the rest of my life. I had to have faith, or there would be no hope. Watching my mother pray with her bible and watching her faith in action, knowing her prayers were answered, gave me the courage to do the same. Going to church each Sunday and to Bible study every Wednesday helped me to believe in a higher power.

In the back of my mind, there was always the thought that, with one slip, I could fall into being a prostitute or a junkie. I had to keep replacing those negative thoughts and keep reminding myself of the goals I had set. No matter what the rest of the world did or said, I was determined that what happened to the ones who did fall and failed to get up and became prostitutes and junkies was not going to happen to me. I lived in a shell. I trusted no one. I feared I would lose control and give in to this life that surrounded me.

I was terrified of becoming just another statistic. I was never going to relinquish my control, not even to God. I soon learned that that was exactly what I had to do, relinquish my control to God if I wanted to be free and escape from all the madness.

As children we weren't treated very well because of the place we lived and because of what my mother did. I was so deeply troubled by that. Everyone knew my mother and what she did. Some of those people thought me and my brothers and sisters would be a negative influence on their children, and they didn't want them around us. People would say things and do things that made us feel very embarrassed. It hurt to think that people viewed us as bad influences.

Instead of being like my mother when she protected us with diplomacy, I vowed to make them all eat what they thought and said about us, eat everything they said ever about us. I was going to show them all that they were wrong about me, that they were wrong about us. It was just a matter of time. I knew, with hard work, a little luck, and perseverance, I could shut them all up. It wasn't easy to be positive and to maintain that way of thinking. It was very hard not to give in under the negative pressure put on us every day, but it just made me more determined.

We were all held responsible for what our mothers did, especially by some family members, but even so, those same family members were there to teach us the importance of having extended family and having high expectations for us as members of the family. I learned to listen even when I didn't want to listen because of the wisdom they possessed; they knew more than I knew. It was like really playing a game of pretend with my relatives, instead of playing with the others in the neighborhood. I was sweet and innocent—because my mother wouldn't have it any other way. She would not allow us to talk about her siblings, not ever. We had to always be respectful to them no matter what they said about us, and they said plenty! They didn't mind that we heard what they were saying. They thought they were talking in code and we wouldn't understand what they were saying.

My younger brother heard my mother say she was tired of them painting these portraits of her children. My brother came to the rest of us and said he was looking for the portraits that our uncles and aunts had painted of us. He didn't understand that they were telling our mother that they didn't want their children around, but I understood just fine. I would have just as soon told them off to mind their own business, but we were taught differently, and our mother wouldn't hear of it. I knew exactly what they were saying about us.

Nonetheless, my mother would say, "These are my brothers and sisters, and I will put them in their place. You all will stay in your place as children." She refused to allow us to be disrespectful to any adult because she knew the values we needed to learn, and she was going to see to it we learned them. Our aunts and uncles would not have stood for the disrespect anyway. They taught us a lot about moral character and core values. I just felt so sorry for the hurt our mother felt because of the way some treated us. Not all of them spoke about us that way, but some of them.

Life was a survival skill each day; you had to wake up every day and apply those skills. It took a lot of practice to learn to lie and manipulate others, getting by day by day just so I could live another day long enough to maybe someday be free of this way of living.

One day, my hope was I wanted to live free, without fear. I wanted my aunts and uncles to stop looking at us as though we were the worst children in the world. I set a goal in my life to prove them wrong and to take the pressure off my mother.

I would never give them any ammunition to look down on my mother or on us.

I would never do anything to give them something negative to talk about. I just would not get caught. I knew it really didn't matter one way or the other. They'd find something to look down on us about, no matter what. They were going to find fault with me no matter what I did or didn't do. I was the oldest, and to them I had a lot of influence, and I did. I was streetwise and smart.

Even so, my goal, my promise to myself, was I would never give them any ammunition or do a single negative thing for them to talk about and hold over my mother's head.

Mrs. Evans and the
Language of Our People

Mrs. Evans was from the south, somewhere in the south Sea Islands, the Gullah Island. Mrs. Evans lived in the back two-room kitchenette apartment. Our mother paid her to watch us when she was gone. She was in her nineties at that time, and she must have been a slave at one time in her life. It was the early 1950s, so she was born in the early 1860s, like my great-grandmother. She spoke with an accent. The standard English way of pronouncing her name was Mrs. Evans, but she pronounced her name "Mrs. E-vins." She fed us sometimes with succotash, a dish made up of corn, okra, lima beans, sometimes meat, and I don't know what else, but it was good, along with some soda, hot water, and corn bread.

As far as keeping us in line went, when we misbehaved, Mrs. Evans would say in Gullah, "Ah'm quian go git mu strop," in that Gullah way that she spoke.

In Standard American English, it would have been "I'm going to go get my strap or belt." I was fascinated with the way she spoke because it reminded me of the way my grandmother, my great-grandmother, and my great-great-grandmothers spoke.

What it *meant* was that she was going to get her belt! Mrs. Evans looked out for us at my mother's request, but I didn't know that then. I thought my mother had just left us alone to take care of ourselves as she always left strict instructions for us to follow.

Mrs. Evans had a son she called Ni-da, who was a guitar player. I clearly remember times when he'd sit on our back porch and play his guitar and sing the Mississippi Delta blues. Ni-da had a sixth finger on his left and right hand. That was how I recognized him.

He was known as the famous Hound Dog Taylor. I did not know he was famous until later when someone was talking about him on the radio and how famous he really was. I thought, *That can't be.* I went to the computer, looked him up, and sure enough, it was him the same man who used to play the guitar on our back porch, the son of the woman who babysat us. I know this because of the sixth finger on his left hand and right hand. He had not changed at all; he still looked like the same man I remembered him to be. I never knew he was so famous until now. I had heard the name Hound Dog Taylor when I was a child, but I didn't know he was a well-known musician leaping from Chicago outdoor markets and ghetto bars to national and, finally, an internationally famous blues icon with a Grammy-nominated album.

There is a website dedicated to him as well. We knew many people like him but were too young to understand what a historical place Bronzeville really was. Ni-Da also had a sister; she and my mother were good friends. She lived in the kitchenette apartment with her mother, Mrs. Evans. Mrs. Evans was a unique woman.

How My Mother Met
the Other Women

My mother met the women in 1952. She was doing their family's hair, hot combing, curling hair for two dollars a head. My mother was also doing the hair of the gay men in the neighborhood every year at Halloween when they attended the Sissy's Ball at the Coliseum in downtown Chicago. No offense to anyone, but that is how they referred to themselves, and that is what they called the ball at the Coliseum in Chicago. My mother also did their makeup and helped them get dressed for the ball they called the Sissy's Ball. They wore gowns and beautiful dresses, some of which came from boosters in the neighborhood—a term I grew up knowing it meant "thieves"— and they stole their dresses and dresses for others. All anyone needed to do was put in their order, and the boosters would go to work fulfilling those orders. It was like a real business, like placing an order online in today's society.

The men attending the ball wore mink coats, evening gowns, and fine jewelry—and lots of them looked as good as any woman did! One year, when I was just seven or eight, my mother was doing Sweet Cake's hair, getting ready for the ball, and he noticed I didn't have my ears pierced. He asked my mother if he could pierce them, and she said yes. He—Sweet Cakes—pierced my ears, doing such a good job, that I never forgot it in all these years. He was gone many years ago. Halloween was the only time gay men or women could legally dress up in drag back then and go outside the neighborhood and be safe.

Once they were beautiful, they would leave our tiny apartment and go right to the Coliseum. They were there to wow the crowds and attract the men. They were quite a sight, but we got the first show of all of them parading around—first through our kitchen and living room, then later when they paraded through the neighborhood. Beverly Ann dressed in a man's suit all the time; she was stunning on the night of the ball. Unfortunately, she was murdered as she ventured outside the community. The circumstances of her death are unknown but surely related to her living as a man in a time when she lived, being clearly unaccepted for her lifestyle.

A while after the women got to know my mother, Mrs. Jackie asked her to hold her money. She said she trusted her. No one would know she had it, so she didn't have to worry about anything happening to her or to her money. My mother did as she was asked, and she paid her well. She also helped my mother with food and rent for a while after she was turned down for welfare. If it had not been for her, we would have been set out on the street with no place to go; every day, women, their children, and all their belongings were set out on the street. It was not uncommon to see all of people's belongings sitting on the street, and it was so embarrassing, but these women would go out and help them collect their things and find a place for them even if they had to take them in themselves. It was our greatest nightmare that it would happen to us. It did happen once to us, and it was so embarrassing and scary, but our mother quickly found somewhere for us to go.

By 1957, they were very close, and the other women of Bronzeville had begun to trust and collaborate with one another. They vowed to see to it that no child or family ever went hungry, needed shoes, wanted for clothes, or was set on the street if they could help it. They began this crusade to save, feed, and take care of the neighborhood. They became dead set on saving the neighborhood from those who were already sucking it dry of money, people, and talent and putting nothing back. This was the moment many of them, my mother included, embarked on a life of crime. This woman showed them how to make the money they needed to survive. She said they could do better by helping everyone because those people "w[ere] going to use that stuff anyway, but they could send them to treatment if and when they wanted to go and help others too."

They didn't have a clue what they were getting themselves into.

Famine to Feast

After my mother started selling drugs and acting as an invisible "safe-deposit box," she was making real money. Suddenly, we got everything we never had before. We moved down the street into a larger apartment because the one we were living in had only two rooms. There were seven of us in those two rooms. The new apartment had *seven* rooms, and for the first time in our young lives, we had our very own rooms. There were no worries about food, clothes, or shoes and certainly not for shelter.

My brother, the one I used to carry around on my hip, shared a memory that we went from having no furniture to having seven rooms of nice furniture, bought from someone for three hundred dollars. That would be roughly three thousand dollars in today's dollars!

But it was an ugly trade-off—and not a trade-off for the better. We now worried about the police kicking in the door. I worried about my mother going to jail. We worried about the stickup man and thieves breaking in, thinking we had something worth stealing. We literally worried about our lives.

We were finally able to get a dog; we could afford one for the first time. The first one was a brown-and-white puppy we named Chico, but he died of distemper. Then I found Blackie in the coal bin in the basement, just below our new apartment. I remember the first time I asked for a puppy. My mama said, "Honey, you know we can't afford no dog. We can't hardly feed us, let alone no dog," and now we were able to have a dog.

Blackie was a black English chow mix, born to a stray dog that had a litter of puppies. I found them on top of a pile of coal in the basement. I took one home, and naturally, I named him Blackie because there was not a speck of any other color anywhere on his tiny body. Blackie was a very alert and smart dog. But he joined the new family business, and he became the lookout dog for the house. He was our protector. We always knew when the police were around because Blackie would alert us, that, like us, he couldn't stand the police. He could smell them coming a mile away, and he barked and barked until he alerted someone in the house. The man who trained Blackie to be an attack dog said it may have been that the dog could smell the animal fat the police used to oil and clean their guns. Rudy trained Blackie to attack without warning. Every time the police came to the house to do a raid, they had to bring the dog catcher's net, but they couldn't catch Blackie.

When the police did catch Blackie, it was because he was with Rudy, a man familiar to everyone in the neighborhood. He had taken a liking to Blackie and taught him a lot of tricks. He was in the hallway, shooting up heroin. When the cops charged into the building, he put the spike and the drugs under Blackie's collar and told him to run. Blackie took off, and they chased him around the back of the building. By the time they caught up with him, Blackie had already shaken off the drugs and the spike along the way. The police arrested him and Blackie, though they didn't take Blackie to the dog pound. They took him to the police station and locked him in a cell next to the man. It was the funniest thing to see Blackie being loaded into the patty wagon and carted off to jail. I guess the police were fed up with Blackie because they could never catch him; he would never let them get into the house.

We got him back, but my mother had to go to the station to get him and pay a fine to get him. That was funniest thing. We had never seen anything like it; however, Rudy remained locked up, and we laugh about that even to this day.

After my mother came home from the penitentiary, she took Blackie to live with her. Blackie died in 1977 after living with us for almost twenty years. He accidentally got locked out of the house in the winter and froze to death one cold Chicago winter's night.

Once we had a new apartment, my mother talked our grandmother into staying with us. She offered to pay her to cook and clean and take care of us. My grandmother kept the money for my mother just as my mother once did for her friend. My grandmother I think was a little money hungry. If she had control of the money, she could spend it on whatever she wanted. She bought the food and paid the bills. Everyone in the neighborhood loved her; they brought her gifts, ice cream. She loved RC Cola and smoked Salem cigarettes. She loved Chicken by the Box, fried oysters from the Queen of the Sea, and polish sausage from the Hamburger Hub under the El tracks.

It was the junkies and dealers who kept her supplied with these things. Other workers and people in the community loved her, and they brought her gifts whatever she wanted. She loved the attention, and she mothered them all, gave them advice, and she always tried to talk them into going to treatment.

Oppressed Oppressing and Providing Them Care and Treatment

The women of Bronzeville were paying for anyone who wanted to go to treatment. Some went to treatment down to Lexington, Kentucky, at a famous—and infamous—place called the Narcotics Farm. It wasn't called that back then, but what I always heard while listening to their conversations them referring to it as Lex. It wasn't until I was doing research on it did that I found out this place that they all talked about was a small hospital on a several-acre farmland adjacent to the State of Kentucky prison. I thought it was an elaborate place (the minds of children)! I found that they did research on drug addiction and they admitted Blacks to the program for experimentation. The Narcotics Farm was a government-funded prison for rehab and research in Lexington, Kentucky, until 1974. Its mission was to understand drug addiction and the addict to find a permanent cure for rehabilitating them. Picture shows the farm in the back behind the cows. Famous people went to the farm for rehabilitation.

A lot of celebrities from all over the country went there for treatment: jazz artist, singers, poets, and writers. It was one of the only places where Blacks could go for long-term treatment.

The addicts would come back, remain clean for a while, and then go right back to using again. It just didn't make sense to me to pay all that money to help them get clean but they go right back to their habit.

When they didn't stay clean, my mother would cut them off, and so would the other women. If they went back to using, the women would still take care of their children but not them. They could no longer get anything from these women as their suppliers and had to go elsewhere.

It made me so angry that I started to think, *What was the use?*

I couldn't figure out why I was living in this vicious circle that just continued and continued to go around and around without stopping. I really wanted off this roller coaster. I hated the ride. We had heroin addicts living with us, driving us to school, and cleaning the house for their fix. This was my mother's way of taking care of them. It was the methodology of the Narcotic Farm. It was the reason the farm was finally shut down in the '70s.

My mother would take care of their children if they didn't have a place to stay. She gave the parents room and board, and they worked for their fix, but they had choices. They could go to treatment and then go home to their own home, which the women set up for them, or home to their parents and family members once they quit. The women would call their families once they were clean to try to get them home, but there was almost never a response; it was like no one cared. I was so confused by that and saddened because many of them had no one who cared. I felt, no wonder they can't stay clean!

It was so uncomfortable and shameful for me to have them drive me to school. Sometimes they would be in a nod, and I was so embarrassed. I was the oldest. I was very much aware of what was going on. I saw all the people she was involved with, the dangerous people she knew and did business with. It made me afraid for her safety and for ours. It didn't occur to me then that they couldn't get out. Later, when I overheard them discussing how trapped the felt, that was when I became even more afraid.

After she had done her time, I knew I only had to worry about old age taking her away from us again. For the first time in my life, since I was seven years old, I thought I had my mother again, and I was not as afraid as I was in the past, but old habits are hard to break. I still worried because she was getting older, and the older I got, the older she got and closer to her time to go. That was the way I ratio-nalized things as a kid; it made me feel better.

She didn't come back home when she got out. She went to live with her longtime boyfriend.

I'd always been protective of my mother. Losing her was my life's greatest fear. I worried all the time about her, even to the point of having anxiety attacks; they got worse over time from the stickup men and the police raids. My mother came from a religious back-ground. Born and raised in the South and in the church, she never drank, smoked, or did any drugs herself. She even wore a mask over her face when she was cutting the heroin. She was strong that way, and she taught us not to put these chemicals into our bodies. Alcohol, cigarette smoke, and drugs would poison the body. So how could she do this and know it was harmful to others?

My Mother: Anatomy and Mindset of the Oppressed

As I was her daughter, my mindset and belief were that my mother's behavior now and then reminded me of someone who had lots of issues. Her behavior mimicked that of someone who had been molested or sexually abused. I knew something was wrong, and my aunts and uncles seemed to me to be guarding a secret, but they would never come right out and say what that secret was. They would allude to something having happened but never would discuss it out right. Every now and again, one of my aunts would say something about something that had happened. But she would never say enough to tell what really happened no matter how hard I tried to get it out of her. My uncle would also get very angry about being asked about my mother and what might have happened to her. I felt that something happened because I often wondered if this behavior was why he was so reluctant to speak about it. I wondered if this was why he never allowed his children to attend family reunions or why all the girls in my mother's family allowed themselves to be beaten and battered by their husbands. These were deep, dark family secrets. The good thing in my memory bank was that I don't remember any of my mother's brothers ever hitting their wives. That does not mean it never happened; I did hear that it did, but I never saw it or indications of it.

My mother was a person who loved unconditionally, although I believe she may have had misplaced priorities due to some of the decisions she made during her lifetime. I have my stories to tell about my mother, some before she became involved with illegal activity. Later stories have led me to believe that something happened to her when she was very young. Some say it had to do with incest, but they won't elaborate. Others in the family may have experienced the same things she did, but it may have been too much for them to discuss. Some say they made a pact never to talk about it; the pact has remained strong all these years. No one has ever told the real story. I don't know what the real story is or if there is a story or if anything happened; no one will talk to me.

Of the three who are left, none of the others seems to be willing to divulge any of the details of what may have happened.

Who knows—maybe nothing happened! But I strongly felt there had to be something. A cousin reminded me that our grandmother cut off from one side of the family. I have my suspicion as to why, but no one would answer my questions as to why. Maybe it happened during the 1860s, when my family was still enslaved, then the story worked its way down to my mother's generation. Maybe, but I know that something happened. As an educated adult today, I recognize the behaviors my mother exhibited were ones exhibited by victims of physical and sexual abuse. It would explain why my mother would never allow anyone to touch us, pick us up, kiss us, or hug us when we were children. She always stood firm on that, and if we allowed that to happen, we got the worst whoopin' you could get; my grandmother was the same way.

They always talked to us about staying away from strangers and not talking to any adult without another adult present. My grandmother didn't allow us to speak to strangers or to be touched by anyone but them. It seemed to be a way of life back then. I wonder if it was because of the things that happened during slavery. Rape was common. Little, if anything, changed even after slavery ended. Growing up, I heard stories like that but was too young to understand. The older I got, the more in tune I was to my surroundings and what was happening, especially having grown up during segregation and during the civil rights movement. Child molestation was very common.

My mother had many men—eight of whom she had children with. All eight of us—I and the seven children I cared for, starting with the time I could walk and take care of myself, had different fathers. None of the rest of my siblings knew it. I did because I knew all of them and their names. I knew all the fathers, but I never told anyone until we were all adults.

My mother was very political-minded. She was into the political process, and she wanted me to be politically inclined as well. She was thrilled to have the right to vote because, at one time in her life, she did not have that right. Her brothers could easily have lost their lives working for the right to vote in Mississippi, where they did so alongside an important leader in the civil rights movement. My mother gave me a membership in the NAACP when I was seven years old, in 1953—eighty-three years after non-White men were given the right to vote, twenty-three years after women were given the right to vote. I was so proud of that membership. My mother told me that, if Democrats were in office, we didn't have to worry about going hungry; there would always be a social program for the poor, jobs program for the jobless, and housing for the homeless. She believed that, if Republicans were in the White House, there would be none of that. The poor would get poorer, the rich would get richer, and there would always be a war, hunger, and no jobs. Even so, she taught me that the right thing to do was to respect the leaders of the free world no matter what political party they were affiliated with. I was always to respect the president of the United States. She also said, if I didn't like what his policies were, I should exercise my right to vote, to vote him out, but never was I to malign the leader of the free world.

My mother wasn't very inclusive in her role as a mother. She didn't do kisses or hugs; she didn't talk about emotional stuff and didn't tolerate weakness. But I knew somehow her emotions were there; the love was there enough for me to know our mother loved us all very much. My mother demanded strength. You had to be strong to earn her respect and her trust, which were the ultimate to her. When I was thirteen years old, I remember asking her why she treated me so differently from my other siblings. It seemed to me they got more attention than I did. After all, I was the one who was taking care of her children! I was strong, and I felt she should have recognized that strength in me. I did everything she asked of me; I tried to please her in every way, but she certainly didn't acknowledge what I had done. I didn't even think she noticed.

Her response to me was "You are the strongest child I have. If something happens to me, I know you will be strong enough to carry out my wishes and take care of my children. I don't need to baby you." Even though I was strong, I was still a child and her child too. I needed her attention, but I guess she was grooming me for what was to come. She knew she was going to jail.

My mother raised her husband's son by another woman, who left him in the hospital; my mother went and got him. When she went to the penitentiary, she left him for me to take care of.

My mother breastfed both his son and my brother at the same time. She fed her baby on one breast and his baby on the other. This was the same boy I helped raised while my mother was in jail. He assaulted me in my bed while I was sleeping. I had undergone thirty-two surgeries to repair an orbital blowout fracture, meaning every bone on the left side of my face was broken, including my scull. My eye was in my face, my eye bone was broken, and there was nerve damage. I had to have implants placed in my face; I was left legally blind in my left eye. My mother was determined she would not allow his son to go to jail. I pressed charges against him and went into the crime victims witness program to prosecute him for what he had done to me. My mother was from the old school and believed in the Black code of ethics, which was you do not tell on each other to the White man, no matter what. It was her experience being raised in the South and witnessing the lynching of Black people living in fear of the White man and never receiving justice.

She was not happy about me breaking that oath or code of ethics; she did not want to see White men sentence him to go to jail as she was. I thought differently although I had seen some of what she had seen. I believed that, if you committed the deed, you should pay for it, especially if you did it to me. She believed that too because that is what she said she was doing, taking responsibility for her crimes and doing the time. I was determined that he was not going to get away with what he had done.

It was always a part of my upbringing that right is right and wrong is wrong and there are consequences for good or bad deeds. Young people in the Black community live by this code and hiding people who are killing and shooting innocent people, but there is something wrong with that concept. Therefore, our neighborhoods are so bad filled with the drugs and gang violence. We as a community do not speak up often enough, and our neighborhoods will continue to deteriorate until we put a stop to it and report it! It is the people who make our communities the way they are by not speaking up. We need to make it known that we will no longer tolerate negative behaviors. Sure, we live in fear of the police, but we also live in fear of the gangs and people in our neighborhood who committee crimes against all our people, which needs to change.

Love and Betrayal

My mother went to court and stood up with her husband's son. She told the judge that we were both her children and she did not want to see him go to jail.

I knew why she did it. She was empathetic to his situation and because she had been in the penitentiary and did not want to see him go, but he had done something wrong and should have paid for it! This was not the first time he had done this' he was a well-known batterer and violent. His own mother had rejected him; my mother was clearly an enabler. He had done the same thing to my younger brother—the same one who was breastfed with him on my mother's breast! He had done the same thing to my youngest sister as a teenager except they were not hurt as badly as I was.

It was hard for me to understand why my mother would continue to protect him.

We were her children. She should have been protecting us.

Her husband's son could really kill someone someday if someone did not intervene. He had come so close to killing me. I had been mere inches from death. My mother continued to push him off on us at every family reunion and gathering. She took him there, and I hated him and her too for pushing him on me and not understanding how I felt. I hated him so much that, this time, I came within an inch of killing him. He had no idea. The only thing that kept it from happening was my cousin was watching me saw me with a knife, grabbed me, picked me up, and carried me off. That was my attacker's lucky day. I knew that one day I would have to forgive him if I was going to heal from my physical and mental injuries.

We had raised him as though he were one of us, but his father made a difference between him and the rest of us. His father treated him better than he treated us, he could do no wrong. After my mother went to the penitentiary, he was stuck with us. We all were going to be split up between relatives, and we fought hard to keep us together. I knew they didn't want us, and the ones who would have taken us in were not able to.

I had just gotten out of the hospital the day before, wearing a patch over my left eye and preparing to go through many more surgeries. My mother was by my side the entire time. I thought my mother would be there for me finally; she took me by surprise. I thought she would stand by me.

I thought she would put me first this time; after all, I was her child! I raised her children while she was gone, and I was her daughter. He was no blood kin at all. Although she was there for me while I was in the hospital, she still stood before the judge and pleaded for him not to go to jail.

I hated her for this. It was one more time she had betrayed me, my brothers, and my sisters, one more letdown.

The lawyers pleaded his case down to a simple assault. He got one year in jail, and he received one year of probation with six months served due to his being in jail six months already.

I was so angry with her for this I called her a bitch and ran out of the courtroom. What hurt and betrayal I felt! What was worse than that was that I called my mother a bitch.

I was feeling the worst and the lowest I had ever felt in my entire life. For that, I could not reconcile myself, because in my mind were the Ten Commandments on my grandmother's refrigerator. In my mind, the clearest was the fifth commandment: "Honor thy mother and thy father." The Ten Commandments were embedded in me; we had to read them every day before opening the refrigerator. This boy broke into my house and assaulted me in my sleep to me; there is no greater violation. After that, I could no longer live in Chicago.

How confusing this was to me! My main question was, why did our mother not have the same respect and concerns for her children that she had for his son? We went through so much growing up, seeing everything we should not have seen and remembering everything that had caused us so much anguish for so many years. I literally felt like the devil was calling me, beckoning to me to go to him.

Who will cry for the frightened little girl?

I remember as a young girl in Bronzeville that there were many gay women, pimps, and drug dealers who were in pursuit of me, wanting to turn me out, this little Black girl with green eyes, hazel eyes. I was so uncomfortable with it, but again there was no place for me to hide. I had to play the game that I would have been captured by, the rules of the game that were set by someone else. I broke all the rules. I was determined that I was the hunter and I was not going to be the one captured by the game. I was forced to learn to survive. I had to be manipulative with the pimps and the dope dealers who preyed on me.

I learned to keep them away from me by playing the game of innocence long enough to get away.

I was a pretty girl, but I didn't think so at that time. I felt so much pressure, and I felt so low and ashamed every day, telling myself I was worthy of better. However, I did not want to get caught up in the lifestyle that seemed to be stalking me every day. Afraid all the time that this life was going to get me or someone was going to die. It was just a matter of time. I was taught to be humble, but how hard it was to be humble without being vulnerable. The irony was, while I was being abused, I was smart enough to slip and slide my way without compromising my beliefs, my morals, my principles, or myself.

I had been taught that my body was the most important thing I had to give to anyone, and I did not just give it away lightly. It had to mean something to me, and the one to get it had to be someone special. I learned that it was a game; it was all about the chase, and as long as you did not give it up, they would be forever chasing it. The minute you give in, it was over, and you lose the game. My game was to keep them interested but to never give in.

I was tired of living this way, tired of pretending, faced with the past. I was always trying to escape from this way of living in fear. Everything that had happened to everyone I loved, my friends and family, who did whatever they had to do to feed their children and feed their habits, doing anything to just survive, was hard for me to accept. The worst fear I had was that I would, at some point in my life, become vulnerable enough to become a junkie or fall prey to any or of all the lifestyles people lived in Bronzeville.

This was an enormous fear for me because I lived with anxiety all my life, holding it in. I was always on the run, too afraid to live my life, always protecting myself. I needed a change as I prepared myself to leave Chicago.

Life has always had its way of getting retribution, or as the saying goes, "The sins of the mother or father are always visited on the children."

That has some truth to it for me because it was surely visited on us after my brother died, and then it was me. I was assaulted six months after my brother was murdered by a Chicago police officer, and then my sister died, her second-born son, Tyrone, died, and her baby son died.

My Sister's Story

My sister was born on Christmas Eve in 1952 in the tiny two-room kitchenette apartment at 4749 Calumet in Bronzeville, where we shared the kitchen and the bathroom. My other three siblings and I were in the next room, listening, and could hear everything going on. Our mother was giving birth, and we could hear her moaning and groaning in the next room. She was in labor, and it sounded like she was in a lot of pain. They did not have doctors come out to deliver babies back then; they had midwives. That night, the four of us all slept in the next room in the same bed. It was the night before Christmas. It was the night Santa Claus was supposed to come, the night we were supposed to get toys, but we got a baby sister instead. Our grandmother and great-grandmother in Mississippi sent our care package just as they did every Christmas, which consisted of a shoebox of raw peanuts; Granny's special cake made with egg white icing, coconut, and stewed apple filling, packed in a shoebox; stalks of sugarcane; coconuts; and as Granny called it, covers for the long, cold Chicago winter nights. Granny and Grandma Lou quilted one for each of us and one for the new baby too. This was the highlight of our Christmas because we knew this may be all that we may have gotten for Christmas, but this Christmas, we got a baby sister too.

We had one bed we all slept in with a cotton-filled mattress that housed bedbugs that bit the blood out of us every night. I remember the bedtime advice "Sleep tight. Don't let the bedbugs bite." Our paternal grandmother lived one block up the street, and she provided

Christmas dinner and a lot of fruit, nuts, and Christmas candy for us at her house.

After our little sister was born, we had a Christmas baby, who made this Christmas the best Christmas present we could have had. It was clear she was a beautiful baby. She was a beautiful person. The older she got, the prettier she was. She surely had the personality to go along with her beauty; she was witty and funny. She would imitate and act out and sing every commercial on the radio and, then later when we could afford them, a TV and a record player. She was quiet except when she was playing LPs and forty-fives given to her by the late great jazz singer Sarah Vaughan.

I remember this because I was so jealous of that. I was the one who was into jazz and loved Sarah Vaughan's music, but she thought my little sister was so pretty.

She loved to dance and sing. We would act out the *West Side Story* every day all day, listening to Sarah Vaughan's soundtrack of the *West Side Story*. Every day she would sing and dance Maria's part in the *West Side Story* to perfection. We had the soundtrack LP by Sarah Vaughan. She had given it to her while in Chicago, performing at the historical Regal Theater. We played her soundtrack, sang, and acted it out every day for months. Sarah Vaughan, a friend of our mother's, she thought our little sister was so pretty she stopped by to see her every time she was in town.

We must have seen the musical at least twenty times, sneaking into the back door of the Regal Theater. My younger sister and I looked so much alike that I even mistook her for me in a photograph she had taken. She was wearing my suit, and I still swear today that it is me in that picture and not her. We both have hazel eyes, though they may be blue or green in different light. People thought it was the oddest thing that two Black girls had green and hazel eyes.

She could have been a movie star if she had a fair chance in life. That is how pretty and talented she was. Even the late, great Sarah Vaughan thought so. She would bring doves of her music when she was performing in town. Sarah Vaughan was one of the greatest jazz singers in the history of jazz besides Ella Fitzgerald.

It was just not fair! Nothing was fair about it. My mother was not there much for her or us when she was growing up, not like she was in the beginning. Before my little sister reached her teens, my mother was gone to the penitentiary, and my sister was pregnant with her firstborn, a girl. Our mother, shortly thereafter, left for the penitentiary.

My sister was just a child herself. I was the closest to a mother she had at the time, and she resented that because I was her sister, not her mother.

She was angry every bit as much as I was, but I was six years older than she was and more experienced in the streets.

She was lost without her mother and was turned out by her boyfriend at an early age in her life.

She was pregnant a second time at sixteen years old and had a son.

She got married to her son's father and divorced him to marry someone else. Her baby's father and his aunt and guardian signed him up for the army when he was sixteen years old so he could try to support my sister and his son. He was deployed to Vietnam. That happened far too many times to young Black men his age. They join the army to earn money for their families and are the first to be sent to the front lines, too young to be fighting a war. He did come back, but he was unstable and had PTSD. He was never the same again. My sister had moved on with someone else, leaving her son with him and his family.

The head of that family and my nephew's guardian passed away, and his father was not capable of caring for him, so he was returned home to us and raised by us and me while she raised her daughter. She later had another daughter by her husband.

She met her husband, married him, and he cut her off from all of us because he wanted to control her. If there was ever someone I never liked, it was him. He was the one who would not accept her son or her family. She did not like the idea that I had taken her son probably because she had to see him every day and was guilty about it, but with my sense of family loyalty, I could not see any other option.

She was looking for love in all the wrong places. She wanted the kind of love she should have gotten from her mother and did not get from her father—none of us did.

My sister turned to drug use. It was a common thing to do in the neighborhood; everyone did it. Kids did not know any better, and it was readily available. Everyone was doing it; we were shut off from the rest of the world, living in segregation and poverty.

The same thing happened to cigarettes, which we now know is considered as a gateway drug and were advertised all over everywhere in our neighborhood signs everywhere. It was just another thing to do that we knew nothing about. Alcohol was the same: advertised all over the neighborhood, and the children thought it was okay or cool to do, once again not knowing the dangers of it.

For my generation, drugs, alcohol, violence, and sex were all about ignorance and a means of escape or a way to get through things that caused you anguish, mental-health issues. It was self-medicating. Everything was there, and we did not know enough about any of it except that it made you look grown-up and everybody did it. As I became older and more educated, I knew it was unhealthy. I quit smoking and drinking. I wish I had known sooner about the effects of all of it, because my kids starting smoking and drinking. Had I not done it, maybe they would not have either. My mother and her siblings never drank or smoked, but some of their husbands drank enough for all of them. We thought smoking and drinking were a way to cope with the effects of racism and poverty. Sometimes, smoking a cigarette could keep a person from hurting someone; it was a way of releasing tension.

My sister did eventually get her son back for a time; he wanted to be with his mother, and as much as it was difficult for me, she was his mother, and he was her son. After about six months, Child Protective Services called me and asked me if I would take him back; the school had reported that he had been beaten by his mother's husband.

While he was there, he started using marijuana at eleven years old. I went to court to get him legally, and he remained with me until his death on January 26, 2005, at which time I removed him from life support. That was the hardest thing I had ever had to do. He died within ten minutes exactly two weeks to the date, after his mother's death on January 12, 2005.

We had just returned from burying her. He loved his mother so much.

She had divorced her husband and moved close to our mother after our mother returned home from the penitentiary in 1971. She became closer to the family after that and began to build a relationship with her son after he became an adult.

She had another child, about fifteen years younger than her first son. She also had another son, but he passed away at ten months of age due to an enlarged heart. That was heartbreaking for all of us, especially for her. It could have been hereditary because her biological father died of a heart attack and she had pulmonary hypertension, which took her life too. My Sister gave her life to Christ on Christmas Eve 2004 and spent her days in the hospital reading her bible.

Her son loved his mother so much that, upon learning about her death while in jail for a petty misdemeanor, he collapsed and was taken to the hospital. Two weeks after her death, I had him removed from life support, hoping and praying that he would survive. I had no idea he was ill as he had never been sick a day in his life except for allergies. I found out at the very last moment that he supposedly had undiagnosed leukemia.

He had never been sick, but when he was about seven years old, I took him in for a physical, and the doctors told me there was something wrong with his testicles, and it would give him problems as he got older. I still don't know what that meant, but I question myself every day about that. I still find it strange that there was never any indication of leukemia, and I think it was foul play. Perhaps he even willed himself to death upon learning of his mother's death.

I became more convinced of this after reading the letters he wrote to me and his mother.

I'd spoken with him by phone for the last time when I'd told him his mother had passed. I always second-guess myself about what would have happened if I had not told him about her and if I waited until he came home. I don't think that would have been right either.

He had the right to know. This was one of those times when one could say "There was nothing you could do" or "You did all you could."

I was glad to find that he had written a series of letters to me and his mother. One was meant to be read at her funeral. I received one letter before the funeral, one after the funeral, and one before and after he died. It was as if he had given up and knew he was going to die. The letters are below in the order I received them.

This was his letter to me:

> Dear Auntie
>
> I hope this letter finds you in the best of health, I pray my letter reaches you before you take off for Chicago to bury my mother, if not please check your fax machine. Losing my mother is the worst thing that could have happened to me it is tearing me apart knowing them drugs is the reason I am in jail and the reason I can't make it to my mother's funeral. Auntie if I had one wish it would be to hold my mother and kiss her and let her know how much I love her.
>
> I turned myself in on December 5th, 2004, thinking that because I was doing so well the judge would take it into consideration and let me go. The bible says you'll reap what you sow. I have been doing wrong for so long and I finally decided to turn myself in trying to do what's right, never in my wildest dreams would I have thought I would lose my mother especially while I was locked up. I can't sleep, can't eat, I even think differently. The only thing that is on my mind is why I couldn't have gotten myself together before she passed away. I can't imagine how you must feel that was your sister let alone how the entire family feels.

Right now, I am on suicide watch I am locked down twenty-three hours a day, it is tough. They say that God doesn't give you any more that you can handle, I can't tell. They say everything in life happens for a reason I don't know about that either. The other day this guy in my cell said if you ever want to talk, he'll be there to listen, first of all he told me to stop weeping and that my mother is in a better place and then he went off into his personal business, he told me he killed his mother, father and his sister and is serving two life sentences. He then stated to me that God didn't want me to go to the funeral God wants me to remember the good times we once had and one thing for sure I'll see her again in heaven, that really touched me. Auntie you can lead a horse to water but you can't make him drink. For years you put your all into me and your son and the whole children. Give yourself credit you have done all you could do the rest is up to us.

My pray today is that each and every one in this world gets ourselves together and make amends to all of those we have harmed before it is too late. To live with the pain and guilt I have inside, I wouldn't wish this on my worst enemy.

This was his letter to his mom:

Dear Mom,

I was going to Bible College and cutting hair in the barber shop. I found I had a warrant and decided to turn myself in on December 5th 2004, which was hardest thing I have ever done. Mom I really decided to turn my life around on my own. I have a beautiful woman in my life and

I have been working very hard to have some kids. I remember you asking me when I was going to give you some grandchildren. Mom I wanted to surprise you and invite you to my wedding once I finished Bible College.

Mom I turned myself in thinking that because I was doing so well the judge would let me go, come to find out if I didn't turn myself in the judge was going to give me five years. Mom for the first time in my life I was beginning to see myself having a successful life. January 12th my case worker came down and said he had some bad news and I needed to call my aunt, my aunt got on the phone and told me what had happened, I couldn't believe what I was hearing and immediately I broke down. Mom, even though we wasn't very close throughout my childhood we had been working on our relationship, mom I never stopped loving you and right now I need you more than ever. Mom I never knew how sick you were every time I talked to you, you said you were fine and doing alright had I known how serious your condition was I would have stopped everything just to be with you. Mom the bible says many are called but there is only a few who are chosen. If I had one wish, it would be to kiss you and hold you and tell you how much I love you. I have no idea how I am going to get through this. This is my worst nightmare to have my mother pass away and not be able to be there to see her last days on this earth and on top of that be locked up. Mom I am very hurt because we never got the chance to sit down and have a mother son talk. The bible says, "You will reap what you sow." I have been doing wrong for so long I never imagined losing my mother the one who brought me into this world being the one thing I would reap.

Life dealt a mean blow to him, so much so that he chose to take on part of the responsibility of his and his mother's relationship, and none of it was his fault just as his mother's condition and problems were not all her fault. The responsibility lies in the circumstances under which we lived, our mother's conditions, and all the things that happened to her. These things were the cause of all our conditions, helping to repeat the same cycle over and over. This is why education is so important. We need to understand the human condition. Some of us had resilience and self-efficacy, and some of us didn't. We all were products of someone else's mistakes and the product of the environment in which we lived.

He told his mother in his letter that was read at her funeral that he would see her soon.

We had no idea how soon.

He was my son too as I'd raised him. I had to take a back seat to his love for his mother because it is a bond that can never be broken even as I watched, as the two of them suffered abandonment, abuse, and addiction.

In his final letter to me:

Dear Auntie,

I want to thank you for being there for me time and time again, I want to thank you for the love you've shown me throughout my life time. Take care of yourself you're the only mother I have ever known. Please pass this message on to your clients and the rest of our family to quit being your parent's biggest disappointment get yourselves together before it is too late, make your parents proud. When you get a chance please tell the family to write me, I need every one's support. Can you send me the obituary in a giant print and one hundred pictures of me and

my mother and the whole family to remind me
of the good times, did my sisters get something
off my mother's body to remind me of her for
the rest of my life. I get out July 4th. I love you
Auntie from the top of your head to the bottom
of your feet. Please write me back today! l Love
you for real.

Love always

He was a troubled child from the time he was old enough to
know my sister was his mother and I was not. He wanted to be with
her, and because he could not be, he needed to hold someone responsible for that.

That someone was me. He always thought I was keeping him
from his mother, but I knew the truth, and I allowed him to grieve
in any way he could. I did not take it personally, but it hurt just the
same.

It hurt because the two of them were in so much pain. If it
could have only been different, I would have made it so. I knew he
would, at some point in his life, understand. It was never for me to
disillusion him about his mother.

I taught him as well as I could to love his mother. I was his aunt
and could never be the mother he longed for. He didn't have her in
life, but he found a way to be with her in death.

He was troubled most of his life, in and out of jail mostly for
petty misdemeanors and drug charges. He started using weed, and
then he moved on to crack cocaine. He stole from me at every turn,
yet I could not turn him away because I knew how he was hurting
inside.

I put him in treatment several times. He put himself into treatment on his own as well. He was someone who had a magical way
of getting people to like him. He had a beautiful smile and a charismatic personality. You could see him coming a mile away, and everyone loved him no matter what he did. He was so much like his uncle
who went before him, practically a reincarnation.

I am so tired of watching so many young people die. I just want people, parents, to understand how making wrong and bad decisions can affect your children for generations to come.

My nephew was just one of many to go early because of the choices of others. I knew he was going to die early just as I knew many others were as well. I have always known there was something about the way I thought about things. Some call it a gift, but I never wanted to think about it in that way because it frightened me.

I would think about people dying and see death on their faces, and it would scare me, and then it would happen just the way I felt it would. I fought it every time. I didn't want to face the reality that I might have some sort of sixth sense, so I remained in denial for years.

Until recently, when I worked with a young man, a young Hispanic boy, a senior in high school, and all I could see was death in his face. I even called his mom and spoke with her, asking her to buy different clothes, to talk to him. I tried to dismiss it, even to the point of talking to him and telling him to change his lifestyle—how he dressed, his thinking, his way of talking, his habits. Nothing worked. I told my supervisor what I felt. I couldn't tell him I felt he was going to die too! I just said, "I am so afraid for him!"

One night, I was watching the news, and a young eighteen-year-old was discovered on the street. He'd been stabbed to death. They didn't mention any names, but I knew with the same surety as I'd known my brother had been shot in the back six times that it was him.

The 1960s

The Bail Bondsman and the Brutality of the Police

When I was a teenager, I was known by the representation of my mother. I was always stopped on the street by the police and searched in the middle of the day. They would stop me on the street; on my way home from school, or while I was just out and about. I could be thrown against a wall and searched just for the fun of it; they knew I didn't know anything. They knew I wasn't a part of any drug use or drug dealings, but they still harassed all of us just because they could. Sometimes I would be so angry, and other times, I would just go with the flow; there was nothing else I could do.

While I didn't know specifics, I knew what my mother was doing was wrong, and I hated it. Even so, it wasn't me; it wasn't my fault. I didn't do anything wrong, and I had no control over what my mother did, nor did the other children who grew up with me.

Certainly, some of the police officers harassed me just to see if I would tell, but I didn't know anything to tell. It made me so angry at them—and to be honest, they were not only picking at us; they were hitting on us as well, trying to go to bed with us, just like the dirty old men on the block. I was conflicted about the betrayal of the police who had no respect for us or regarded themselves as police officers. I was mad at her too—but I knew they were just trying to get a rise out of her. Others wanted cash from her, bribes to make sure they looked the other way. I couldn't understand then why they wanted to hurt her at my expense. In my eyes, they just created themselves as dirty cops, which was the real Chicago story! Full of corruption.

Watching the wrong the police did and them getting away with it were killing my heart. In some cases, they were worse than the thugs and people they were arresting. The words on their badges made their every action a lie—they did not "serve and protect." They were on the take, liars, abusers, thieves, and worse than the criminals they were supposed to pursue. They had it both ways; take the money, and make the arrest. This has gone on for so many years and is still going on not just in Chicago, but across this nation.

Some of them were so bad, they were given names that suited their characters, like the TV personalities, such as Starsky and Hutch in the 1970s police TV drama. One police officer that "earned" his name, was Two Gun Pete (he mimicked the wild old Western cowboy movies; he wore two guns in his front side holsters, drawing them on people like he was a cowboy in the Wild, Wild West). He once killed a man for sport and put notches on his gun to show how many men he killed. The paper said he had killed eleven men, and he confessed to twelve. I saw him in the neighborhood all the time. He once told a man, "When I come back, you better be gone." He turned around and then turned back around and said "I'm back" and shot him. Two others were a pair of characters, as I remember. I don't know if these are their real names, but they were terrifying to me, the fact that they were tall, big African American men, and the way I saw them treat people on the block scared me to death. I remember their big feet—sizes 15 and 16 shoes. They used to kick women prostitutes in the back, take their money, and then lock them for soliciting for sex. They did this to anyone they encountered. I hated them back when I was small, about seven or eight years old. I was terrified of them.

There were two men: Lock-'Em-Up and his partner. They weren't any better than the ones I experienced when I was little. Lock-'Em-Up got his name because he locked up everybody no matter what, even if they had done no wrong. He and his partner were rough and tough and dangerous just like the rest of them. Unfortunately, his partner's wife shot him several times, which left him paralyzed from the neck down. I remember hearing people say it was because he had physically abused her, just as Two Gun Pete's wife shot him for abusing her. I read this online in a newspaper clip. Lock-'Em-Up arrested me on several occasions for nothing more than being my mother's daughter or just walking down the street. Finally, a judge forbade them to touch me ever again unless they had probable cause to do so. The order came because on my seventeenth birthday on June 2, 1963, as I was going to a dance hall called the Peps for teens to celebrate my birthday. They stopped me and beat me, trying to make me tell on my mother. I instead ended up in the hospital with a ruptured kidney. They had kicked me down a flight of stairs inside the police station at Forty-Eighth Street station near Wabash Avenue. They hit my girlfriend and caused her to go into labor after they slapped her and threw her into the paddy wagon. She was taken to the hospital, where she gave birth to a baby girl. They arrested me and eighty other teens who were trying to protect me and charged all of us with race rioting and inciting to riot. Chicago was very volatile at that time with race issues especially with the civil rights movement in full swing. They did their dirty deed and tried to cover it up, as per usual, and transferred me from one institution to another and to the hospital without notifying my mother until she hired a lawyer to track me down and his bail bondsman to get me out.

My life changed once again when I was introduced to the mob by an attorney who was a Mafia lawyer and his Mafia bail bondsman, whose office was in Oak Park, Illinois. That was about ten miles west of the city. The police kept transferring me from place to place to allow me to heal before I went before a judge. I knew this was some big-time stuff. I just didn't know how big-time. I could not believe how it came to be that I was involved with organized crime. The lawyer and his bail bondsman obtained a writ of habeas corpus—which was a judicial mandate to a prison official, ordering that an inmate be taken to the court so it can be determined whether or not that person is imprisoned lawfully and whether or not he/she should be released from custody. With the help of the attorney in downtown Chicago, the bail bondsman petitioned to get me out of juvenile detention. I was released and allowed to go home because I was illegally detained.

What my mother didn't know was that she had sold her soul to the devil and almost me too by getting in bed with these people.

Five months later, the bail bondsman was murdered—shot in the head gangland style and stuffed in the trunk of his car in November of 1963. This happened around the same time our beloved president John F. Kennedy was assassinated, November 22, 1963. At that same time, a Black organized-crime figure I knew well from Bronzeville was shot and killed in a shootout with federal agents on the Dan Ryan Expressway on Chicago's South Side at Fifty-First Street. That year, the month of November was historic in many ways. In Detroit, Malcolm X gave his "Message to the Grassroots," and later, Kennedy's assassin was murdered. In Chicago, an all-out war broke out as several crime figures were murdered. I didn't know why, but I was scared senseless because I knew or had met at one time all those who were murdered, including a well-known mobster I knew.

The bail bondsman had a little black book with all the names of the people he had done business with. My name was in it, and federal agents, as well as other people, were interested to know why. I knew it was only because of him and the La Salle Street lawyer who got me out of jail, but I was scared anyway. I had no idea what was going on. I didn't know what was happening around me; things were happening so fast, and I was in the midst of so much unlawfulness, so much against my teachings and the teachings of the Bible. This was a very scary confliction at its best.

The man I knew was a large man of Italian descent: had black hair, a pot belly, a calm personality. He seemed to be a nice man. He was found shot in the head, slumped over the steering wheel of his car at Fifty-First Street and the Outer Drive South. I thought, *Who would want to kill him?* As it turned out, he too was also connected to the La Salle Street attorney, who was a very powerful man and deeply connected. The attorney eventually became an Illinois supreme court judge. Years later, he was indicted for racketeering and fixing cases and was sentenced to prison for twelve years, dying shortly after his release. I met him in June 1963. He was a handsome tall man, an Irishman with wavy blond hair and blue eyes. I thought he was the most gorgeous man I had ever seen. I didn't see many White people back then. I was only seventeen when I met him. Segregation was supposed to be ending, and the civil rights movement was in full swing, yet where I lived, there were no White people, and we had just gotten our first TV set. The only White people we saw were the firemen, EMTs, social workers, or the police. Yes! I was mesmerized by this handsome tall man and his surroundings, visiting his plush office in the luxurious tall building in Chicago's downtown on La Salle Street.

There were many police officers patrolling our neighborhood. There were so many I could not keep count.

Police officers, several of them, were convicted of charges of taking bribes, murder, and drug distribution in the 1970s and sent to prison. Two other officers were the better of all the police in the neighborhood. They had compassion for the children, and they were not dirty cops. They did their jobs with respect and dignity. They never tried to exploit us, and they had as much compassion for us in our circumstances as they could.

Cagney and Lacey, nicknames for two White female vice police officers, were given their names because of they were as tough as any male officer, just like those in the 1980s TV series *Cagney and Lacey*. They were not on the take. Anyone—White or Black—should have been wary of them because they were there to do their jobs. If they caught anyone dirty, you could bank on them going to jail. Batman and Robin, two White vice officers, got their names because one was short and one was really tall. They had a way of sneaking up on people when they least expected it.

Fear and Mistrust of the Police

I was as much afraid of the police as I was of the pimps, whores, hustlers, drug dealers, and gangsters in the neighborhood.

The police in Bronzeville were as bad as the criminals they constantly sought after and arrested. In my experience, the cops were sociopaths: vindictive, violent, sadistic, and dishonest. Black children in Bronzeville—or anywhere, for that matter—hated and mistrusted the police. In our experience, the police lied to us, locked up our mothers and fathers, and placed children in a social services agency. They lied to the children, used them for their own gain, told them, "Everything is going to be okay if you tell us what we want to know." They never kept their word. The children remembered those lies. It created a deep mistrust of the police. When the police were called to the community, almost always, someone ended up dying or hurt. There was little respect on either side.

This mistrust has always been a part of the Black community. It goes back a long way in our history—all the way back to slavery. When it came to interacting with the law, when the enforcers were involved, someone usually died. The fact was that there were more ambulances in our community than there is any other motor vehicle. It seemed like every day someone died because of the lies, deceit, and violence. It might have been better if they had just told the truth and said what they really wanted. They might have just threatened what they were going to do to the children. That would have been better than lying. The lies built up the children's hope and then let them down, crushing their innocence. The way they treated children was cruel. Children saw every day the harm the police did in the community. Why should we have trusted them then or now?

Why did the cops lie to the children? Why couldn't they have done what they needed to do without involving the children? They would tell the children, "Tell us where the stash is, and we will let your parents go."

Most of the children did not know that information. The neighborhood did not trust the cops—or anyone, for that matter. The motto "Protect and serve" did not apply to us and never did and still does not to this very day. They knew that, if they told, they did it in vain. The cops were lying. The children kept their mouths shut and watched; they knew that the police were not honest, and we hated them more for it. It was total abuse and mistrust. They had the power; we had none.

I was one of the watchers and would never tell—even if I knew something. I knew they were never to be trusted. Some of the police we knew used drugs, were thieves, lied, and abused people in the neighborhood. The only difference between the police and the people who lived in Bronzeville was that the cops always got away with their dishonesty. People were afraid to report them or complain about them because of the threat of retaliation. Everyone knew what would happen to them if they complained. There is evidence of that, we all knew it, it was what we heard and saw—the police killed people in the neighborhood and got away with it. No one would have believed us anyway because we were poor, Black, and had no recourse. If I had known that they would eventually be caught and would do prison time, maybe my life would have been different. In the1970s, police officers went to jail for drug possession, bribery, extortion, and finally, for murder.

I only knew what I saw. My mother never let me know what she was doing, but I saw things she did not know I saw. My mother would never allow me to know that part of her business. I could not tell the police anything for sure even though I saw a lot, being the observant little girl I was. She would prepare the heroin she sold by mixing it with milk, sugar, and quinine, sometimes Dormin sleeping pills, and Ritalin, bagging it up in tin foil and sometimes putting it in the capsules remaining from the sleeping pills. They sold for a dollar a capsule, but she would never allow me to know where she stashed her merchandise, and she certainly did not know I was peeping and listening to everything. Ritalin was sold over the counter back then with no prescription needed. Junkies would use it to keep from feeling sick when they didn't have heroin. People would use it to get intense feelings of well-being, elation, happiness, excitement, and joy. This was something that anyone in Bronzeville could get when needed without a prescription. They used it when they could not get heroin. It kept them from getting sick when they did not have the money to buy heroin. Heroin back then was an epidemic, and here we are seventy years later, and heroin is on the rise in this country again. I always said when I was a little girl, "Why can't people see what is happening to us? And those who brought it into our neighborhood from their safe suburban neighborhoods, it will happen to you." Not only did it happen to the women of Bronzeville who lost their children to drug use then; now the drugs are rampant in the suburban areas across this nation. It is now White kids who are addicted. When will we learn? Is the money worth losing so many lives?

Motherless Children

My education was put on hold when my mother went to the penitentiary in 1968. I was eighteen and left to take care of my brothers and sisters and could not pursue my education. That was just another obstacle that stood in my way, and it prolonged my life in this miserable game I had to play. This game was deadly serious and almost cost me my life. I learned quickly that there was only three ways to go in life: dead, six feet under; go to jail; or walk the straight and narrow. I chose to walk the straight and narrow. I promised myself no one was going to make any choices for me. I was and always wanted to be in control of me and my destiny.

I was arrested many times just because I was my mother's daughter but never charged with anything. The police wanted me to give them information about my mother. I didn't know anything about anything, so they beat me and arrested.

Many people were being killed; didn't life mean anything to anyone? The Ten Commandments said, "Thou shalt not kill." Was I so naive to believe it? This is what I have been taught, and if my grandmother would have known, she would never have stood for this. These women granddaughters of slaves and sharecroppers from the South were no longer invisible women; they are now criminals.

In 1964, my mother was busted along with the other women of Bronzeville, and for the first time, they would be convicted. None of them were invisible from this moment on. They were arrested on charges of conspiracy to distribute controlled substances and being in possession of marked money. This wasn't true; the marked money was found in a crap game where everyone had traces of the marked money on their hands. Everyone who had traces of marked money on their hands went to jail; they were set up. They did their time in a federal penitentiary. I was in my late teens and was thinking about leaving Chicago.

Suddenly I knew what needed to be done; otherwise, who was going to take care of my younger sisters and brothers?

My mother didn't want me to get her out on bond; she wanted me to take that money and take care of her children. But there wasn't much left; they spent an enormous amount of money taking care of other people's children, sending them to college and junkies to treatment, and paying off the police. She stayed in until some friends who owed her money finally bailed her out.

She was out for two years before her sentence was handed down: twenty-one years in prison. She was to serve seven years on three counts of conspiracy, which would run concurrently. She would do seven years in the federal penitentiary at Alderson, West Virginia, and maybe out before that on good behavior. She would have plenty of company because the other women of Bronzeville were also sentenced to seven years at the same federal penitentiary long before Martha Stewart was there.

All four of them went together to Alderson to serve their time and were confined to the same cottage for the duration of their incarceration. They were released early on good time for good behavior. One was out first, and the rest were released shortly after her. I went to see her once she was released to see how she was doing and to get an update on our mother's well-being. I often wondered if they understood what a mess they left behind and what they did to all of us. I can only speak for me and how I felt because it seemed that none of the children of these women felt the way I did. Only Billy, whose mother was the first one out, had the same anger I had. Did they know how much we suffered and how we would continue to suffer with them gone?

How were a bunch of motherless children supposed to survive?

I guess their daughters would have to step up and live up to their mother's reputation and expectation. I remember them saying that they were grooming us for what was to come. My mother went so far as to tell me I was the strongest of all her children and that she knew I would see to her children being taken care of.

Billy and his sister would be left to do the same.

The others and my younger brother were out on the street, strung out; our other friend's mother had passed away. She died before she was to go to prison. Her oldest daughter took over the responsibilities of her sister and all of us in the neighborhood.

The 1970s

The Blessing of Family Reunions

In July of 1976, I had fond memories of that year. We all went down south to Mississippi. It was our twenty-ninth annual family reunion. It was going to happen over the Fourth of July, as it did every year on the week of the Fourth of July; the bicentennial of the signing of the Declaration of Independence, but that wasn't why we celebrated. We celebrated the independence from slavery that day because it wasn't the independence of my people. My people were still slaves and treated like subhumans; it was the independence of the thirteen White colonies. The Fourth of July meant something different to my family and Black families around the country. It was a time for family unity, to come together and celebrate one another. It is and was a tradition to bring back and unite family members who migrated north, to celebrate those who came before us and sacrificed, so much so that we could be free, to set a standard of loyalty, trust, and family unity for us all.

When we traveled, we traveled at night from Chicago to Mississippi, a twelve-hour drive. I often wondered why we traveled at night or in the wee hours of the morning. I later learned that my mother didn't want to travel during the day because it was not safe; it would put us in sundown towns at sundown, which meant that if Blacks were found going through any town after sundown, anything could have happened to us. She preferred to travel after sundown, more toward midnight, when people were asleep due to Jim Crow, and arrive in the morning, when it would be safer. My mother traveled with the *Green Book*, a very important guide for Black people to places that were safe for us to stop and buy gas.

My granny was still living in those days and would be up worrying all night until we arrived. That was what made the trip so special going to Mississippi for the family reunion, taking the risk to see Granny. We knew Granny loved us, and knowing she would be so happy to see all of us made it worth it all. That made me proud, excited, and happy to go see her too.

It wasn't until after 1965 that we were able to drive down south and stop at rest stops and lunch counters to get food and use the restroom. Things were still by chance but much safer than before; we no longer had to use the bathroom by the side of the road, which was dangerous in the middle of the night. We could have been arrested, or something much worse could have happened. We still packed our lunch in a shoebox, of cake and chicken. To drink, we had Kool-Aid in a gallon milk bottle, the same as we did before. It had become a tradition. Before, it was necessary, and now it is by choice.

We all drove down that year, which was always a treat. We were city folk, especially us kids, and seeing the animals on the farms and stopping at the rest stops and talking with others who were going down for their family reunion was a major adventure. While on the highway, it was exciting and thrilling to see cars from all over the United States with different license plates from different states going south for their homecoming. I imagined they were all going back to their roots, going home for their family reunion. I took a lot of pride in that. It was a cultural pride we had in who we were and what that represented. On Black radio all the way from Chicago to Mississippi in every state we passed through, they played the Original O'Jays song "Family Reunion."

It was like everyone in the south was anticipating the arrival of their family from the north. They would get to see everyone again. You could smell the barbecue in every state you passed through. When we stopped at a rest stop, we met people who would say "Y'all going home for y'all's reunion?" and they would say "us too," and we would chat about the reunions going on in every part of the south during the Fourth of July week and how it was so exciting and meant something so special; it meant cultural pride.

Picturing Granny sitting at the kitchen table, wearing her floppy blue hat and matching shirt, full apron on, preparing food for the whole family, was a picture that is etched in my mind and heart forever. Granny baked her most famous Granny cake, a yellow cake with egg white icing and stewed apples, made with two different kinds of cake flavor, adorned with coconut and made from scratch. Granny know she could cook some chicken and dumplins, chicken dressin', potato salad, fried chicken, greens, fried okra and string beans, while the men manned the grill, cookin' the ribs and chicken and other meats. All the girls, all cousins taking turns working in the kitchen, helping Granny or playing bid whist, a Black card game, in the yard.

Granny raised ten children and had sixty-nine grandchildren, twenty-nine great-grandchildren, and six great-great-grandchildren at that time. As long as Granny was alive, our reunion remained in the south. In 1982, our family reunion was dedicated to Granny. Granny received a letter from every elected official of the state of Mississippi, congratulating her for being the head of the oldest living family in Mississippi. Granny passed away just two years later in 1984 at the age of ninety-seven years old. It seemed like she was ready go; she had outlived her husband by thirty-four years, and the day before she passed, she laid out the dress she wanted to be buried in and paid for as many flowers she wanted. Just eleven years prior, her mother, who was once a slave, passed away at 106 years old. I was twenty-six years old at the time of her passing.

Our family had a common history, common with others in the south. We all had Black pride, and we had Black privilege. Black privilege is growing up Black, knowing who you were, knowing where you came from, and being proud of it. We were proud of our slave ancestors who came before us and those who died for us so we could live and be free.

The pride our family had we got from my aunts and uncles, our mother, and grandmothers; they carried it with them all the time. They spoke it, drank it, walked it, lived it, and passed it on to us.

They were so proud of who they were and did not allow Jim Crow or any other Crow to take that away from them. They did not like the way my mother lived her life in the north; some of them were weary of who we were, but my grandmother was not. She loved us unconditionally and was always happy to see us! My mother did not seem to care what the rest of her brothers and sisters thought. She would take us to Granny's house, where she knew we would be welcome, or we went to my uncle and aunt's house. They had a lot of children and gladly opened their doors to my mother and her eight children even if it meant we all slept on the floor, but we knew we were welcome, and somehow that made it all good.

Some of them found fault with me and my brother; we were the oldest for a long time. I thought it was because I was my own person, but by then—I was a teenager—I'd figured out it was because they didn't trust their children around me. I did not care. I did exactly what my mother wanted me to do, and that was to respect them anyway. I did have a powerful attitude. I showed my attitude even more so when I was with them. I was so sure of myself, of who I was, and full of pride. I wanted them all to know I had nothing to be ashamed of. I couldn't control anyone but me. I had some influence with my siblings; we were good and respectful children, contrary to others' beliefs. I was going to defy them by being successful. I knew they still had expectations of us and was always ready to follow through with family expectations. Even so, I knew they loved us, and they set examples for us and set expectations for us.

Reunion Trouble

My sister and I went out one night to a bar with two of our male cousins. We did not know where we were exactly, but a little after we got there, my cousin disappeared. He was supposed to be going to get drinks. He was gone a long time. He was gone too long, and my first thought was to go find him. I got up to look for him, but just then we heard a commotion outside. My sister and I, along with my other male cousin, went to look. Two or three people had him on the ground, and they were pounding on his head with their fists. All I knew was that it had nothing to do with us. Even so, we couldn't allow them to continue to keep beating him, so I went and got my sister and another cousin, and we went out to help, and after getting tire irons out of the truck, we ran to his rescue. I never learned what the fight was about, but you can bet that, as it turned out, it was my fault. My aunts and uncles figured it had to be because of me, the city girl. I was my mother's daughter. To add insult to injury, the truck we were riding in was my aunt's truck. The next morning, she found weed in her truck. Everyone, it seemed, in Mississippi had a microwave and a pickup truck. Anyway, I knew it fell out of my other cousin's pocket. When my aunt got in and picked up his jacket, the weed fell out.

According to my aunt, it had to belong to me, but it was not mine, then I was supposed to tell her whom it belonged to, but all I said was it was not mine. I did not smoke weed. Besides, we had just saved my aunt's son from a beatdown! Yet somehow the weed and the beatdown were the fault of my mother's children! My cousin had flown all the way to Mississippi from Chicago with his parents on an airplane with weed in his pocket, and they never suspected a thing! We had to drive the twelve-hour distance because we could not afford to fly, let alone buy some weed. I would have never done that anyway, not with the way I felt about our family and the respect for them I had.

Out of respect for them, I just said, "It ain't mine because I don't smoke weed." Instead of outright telling on him, I said, "Someone flew down here on a plane with that stuff." If it were mine, I would admit to it. I don't do anything I can't tell anyone about," and I didn't say anything more.

I was defending myself once again and was just plain tired of it, when not only I, but also my cousins, knew I was doing none of those things I was being blamed for. I'd never even been in trouble. They all did their deeds but never stepped up; to me that displayed a lack of integrity. My aunt did not understand that it was their kids they needed to worry about; they were the ones getting into trouble. I knew what trouble was, and I lived in it every day, I saw it every day of my life, and I wanted none of it. I would have never done something like that out of respect for them and for me and for my mother; that is what we were taught, how to stay away from trouble. I was determined to make them regret, someday in the future, all they had accused me of doing. I would make them eat every negative word they ever said about my mother, my siblings, and me.

That day did arrive when my uncle told me that my mother would be proud of me. I was with a group of students on a civil rights tour through the South and went to Jackson, Mississippi, to visit the historical Jackson State University, and he invited my family to join us for dinner.

The Mentality to Survive

Before that and after that, my mother was always defending us when there was no reason for her to have to do so. We would never do anything that she needed to explain to her brothers and sisters or that required her to defend us. My siblings and I had enough to worry about just trying to stay alive without having to worry about doing things that would get us in trouble. We all lived in fear for most of our lives. We feared for our mother's life and safety every day, as well as the safety of our friends and their families. There was always some danger lurking just around the corner. The fact is that we just got used to it. We learned to play the game. What else could we do? We never had a chance to imagine that there was a way out, but we kept hoping. There was no way out. We realized we had to create a way out through hope and faith.

I did not know what it was going to take to get out, but I always knew I was going to get out, and once I got out, my siblings would follow. I had faith that someday I would leave Bronzeville and this way of life. I dreamed that one day I could live like normal people did, like the people on the TV shows we watched as children did— like those people in *Father Knows Best*, *The Donna Reed Show*, or *Ozzie and Harriet*. We never pretended we were them, but we sure dreamed of a better life.

The love-hate relationship I had with the way I lived as opposed to what I was taught in the church caused conflict in my life every day. Even church in my life was a conflict.

Honestly, I am very glad today that I had the church and religion in my life then; otherwise, I would not have survived. I do not believe that people understand the value of the church. If more young people went to church, we would not have so many doing so much wrong and believing in nothing.

Neither the place where we lived nor the people were bad. It was the circumstances and the environment in which we lived. We had to learn to survive the things we saw, and it was way too hard for any child to be exposed to the violence, drug abuse, prostitution, and crime and be expected to live through it all without harm. According to statistics, we probably were not expected to survive; we were destined to be a statistic, and most of us were already statistics. I was determined it was not going to be me. I was not going to be a statistic. I was determined not to be a teenage mother, a teenage drug addict, or a prostitute. I was not one of those to see what drugs did to others and then turn around and say "I see drugs are killing you, so give me some too. I want to die like you." I was not weak, nor was I a follower.

The biggest problems in the neighborhood were the behaviors. Most people did whatever they had to do to survive; some did what they wanted to do no matter whom it hurt. You would have to be there to understand. People who were living a better life than us would say "Pull yourself up by your bootstraps!" or "You aren't trying hard enough!" I heard that enough times, but there were no bootstraps to pull up because we didn't have shoes. None of the adults understood the necessity and the concept of meeting young people where we were to help us. It should have been the other way around, but in our community, no one had anything to give, but they shared what they had. People could not help themselves; they were caught up just like my mother and the other women in Bronzeville were. We could not get out of our lives! That made all of us vulnerable to all the wrongdoings and goings-on in the community. We had little trust and very little hope for life getting better.

I know hope is a powerful emotion; you can't touch it, and you can't color it. Together, hope and faith can conquer almost everything, but if you do not have faith, you cannot have hope. It was a terrible, vicious cycle. Many did not have hope, and they had very little faith, which made it very hard for them to have a vision of a better future. Many gave in to temptation, fear, and despair.

We had a church-based upbringing, and I do believe that being in the church had something to do with my resiliency and my sibling's resiliency. I remember when I thought I was losing my way, I would began to pray, "Lord, please help me. I know you did not mean for me to live this way. Lord, please show me a way out, me and my family." I am so glad we had to stay in the church! If we didn't to go to church on Sunday and on Wednesdays to prayer service, we didn't go outside to play, and there was no TV or radio. I believe that is what gave us the strength to overcome our environment. We were more afraid of our grandmother and our mother than we were of the police, the dope dealer, the gangs, or the prostitute. We knew what we had coming if we disobeyed; we had respect for our mother and our grandmother and did not want to disappoint them. I would rather have had a whoopin' than to see a look of disappointment on my mother's and grandmother's faces. Church gave us something to believe in; it gave us hope and faith. Most did not attend church in our neighborhood the way we had to, and I am sure that going to church is the reason we survived. Young people do not have much of that these days. It is high time that parents recognize that young people need that to grow up healthy and strong in body, mind, and soul with a good sense of who they are.

Mama Coming Home

When my mother came home from the penitentiary, she never talked about her experience, nor did she speak about my grandmother's death while she was gone. I could not relate to her on that level because I did not know how to talk to her. I didn't know how she felt about everything that had happened while she was gone. I could not talk to her about raising her children, the struggles we endured, and the things I had to face during her absence. I had to help feed and clothe all of us and set an example.

My mother and I were not able to communicate with each other now and not for a long time. For me, it was because of the anger I felt inside. She could not speak to me because of all that she had experienced while in prison and all I had experienced while she was gone.

We all had issues because of her being gone and us growing up without a mother for such a long time. When our mother came home, she was free of all illegal activities. I commend her for never doing anything wrong ever again. She could have held animosity for the woman who set them all up for a sting operation and then testified against them in court. This woman was the reason my mother and the other women went to the penitentiary. The woman was also someone my mother had taken care of for many years and trusted her. The ones you trust the most are usually the ones who betray you.

They hated what she had done but did not hold a grudge against her. They just wanted to live in peace and go on with life once they were released. Getting out within days of each other, they came back changed women; they came back to families they had left behind years earlier.

My mother decided to move once again; she found a new place and settled into a northern suburb of Chicago with her longtime friend. The friend owned many properties there, and my mother went to work as an assistant nurse for many years until her retirement in 1990 after a major stroke.

New Beginnings

She was a model citizen from the day of her release and ever after. The lifestyle she found north of the city afforded her more of the lifestyle she had always wanted. She continued to help others and took in women and children who were in need of a place to stay until they could get on their own feet and are able to care of themselves.

She had not come from a background of crime but became a part of it in Bronzeville out of necessity. In the beginning, she would not know anything about drugs or pimps and hustlers, nor did the other women of Bronzeville. They all came from the segregated South in deeply rural areas of Mississippi. Down in the country, this kind of thing did not exist! Drugs, hustling, and theft in the North were just a means to an end, a way to survive; they had to learn to live in the fast lane. At the very height of her time, sometimes we did not see her for weeks. She may have been with her friend. Po John is what he called himself; he was her longtime common-law husband from about 1952 until they got married in 1959. Common-law marriages were very common in those days and recognized in the eyes of the law even though a couple had not registered their relationship as a civil or religious marriage. Though he was not my own father, he was sitting and waiting for her to come home too. He stayed and helped take care of us, and I respect him for that. He was not an educated man, and he had his own demons. He was never raised by his own mother and was not treated very well by his stepmother and siblings. I was taking care of the children day and night while our mother was out trying to get money to feed us. Prison was the one thing that finally took her away from all that. The new life she found in the northern suburban area of Chicago gave us a new beginning away from all the chaos. People have gone to the penitentiary and return to repeat the same behavior, maintain the same friends, and act as if nothing had changed. Change doesn't work that way. Everything had to change friends, behavior, places, and I was proud of my mother for leaving her old life behind. I believe it was the beginning of a healing process for all of us. We had struggled for so long with the conflict of what was right and what was wrong and the guilt and shame in conflict of what we had been taught and what we saw in contrast to each other. We could now focus on being successful, living a normal life, and getting the drugs out of our lives and out of our family. We will never forget because we lost something so very precious that we could never get back, something we would never see or feel ever again. We lost our innocence!

Reflections of the Era of the '70s

At the height of the civil rights movement from the '60s, Bronzeville was on the verge of falling, ravaged by drugs, gangs, violence, abuse, and prostitution. What could I do but ask this question, "What did we ever do to deserve this?"

We were nearing the end of the Industrial Revolution, and the housing covenants were breaking down. Black men in the sixties were working and making a living wage. They were working in the steel mills, the factories, and the packinghouses. By then, Black families were able to educate their children and able to send their children to college and buy a nice car and a home.

By the 1970s, it was all coming to an end; jobs were being shipped overseas, especially in the steel-mill industry. It was happening by design. Black men were being displaced from the working class, and Black women were replacing them by design once affirmative action was in place. The system could hire a female and a minority female and kill two birds with one stone and didn't have to hire a Black man, which ultimately led to the breakup of the Black family.

John F. Kennedy, Robert F. Kennedy, Dr. Martin Luther King, and Malcolm X—all were murdered. I was suffering from PTSD. I felt as though I were going die too because everyone around me was dying. I did not want a life like this; all I wanted was to find a way out.

I thought about suicide, but I had already survived everything that had been thrown at me. I guess I was too strong to go down without a fight.

A Better Way

I finally sat down and determined what it was I needed to do. The first thing on the agenda was I needed to go back to school. I figured out the only thing that would change my life would be to go back to school, and no one was going to stop me or make me feel ashamed, inadequate, or guilty ever again.

I prayed every day that I would have the strength to do what I knew I had to do. I would no longer be afraid that I would lose my way, my culture, or the ways of my people. I refused to give up my heritage and the richness of my culture—including the language I learned as a child. I was still alive, and there must have been reason for that. God must have had a plan for me because I am still here despite everything that had happened to me, even coming close to death, not just on one occasion but on several occasions.

When my mother came home, it was time for me to move on for many reasons. I needed to get away from my mother and everything that was familiar to me to find out who I was and to figure out who she was.

I felt my mother had misplaced priorities; she had never put me first. I would have to return to school and resume my education to make my way out of this life of turmoil. I was the kind of kid that, if someone said to me "You'll never amount to anything!" I would reply "Watch me!"

I was determined to make them eat those words. No one had control over me, and my mother felt there was not room for two women in her house. She told me to leave, and I was determined that I was not going to fail. I enjoyed proving people wrong. For many young people today, if I were to repeat those words to them, they would say "Okay, I'm not going to be anything." They would try to prove you right—while, at the same time, believing it was going to hurt you and not them, not knowing it was the other way around. They only hurt themselves with that attitude. The one thing my mother did teach me and pounded into my head for as long as I can remember was the importance of an education.

That was not me! I was going to prove everyone wrong, but to do it, I knew I had to leave town and start all over. After all the surgeries to repair the damage from my attack, I was prepared to leave. Before I could leave town, I needed to contact everyone who was still alive and whom I had grown up with. I needed to ask them how they felt about the way we grew up.

I needed to know if anyone felt the way I did and how they reconciled with it. I thought it would be therapeutic for me. Knowing how they felt about the way we grew up in the neighborhood would give me the fuel I needed to process what happened to us. I think we all thought it was normal at that time. I needed to talk about it. I needed to know. I needed to get some better answers because it did not feel normal to me.

I needed to talk to my mother about how and why she got started. I wanted to understand what she was thinking and what it was she did not understand about how her actions affected her children. Right now, that would have to wait until I first dealt with the shame and guilt I carried around on my shoulders. I needed to like myself. I needed to figure how to get rid of the shame and guilt and to build my confidence. That meant leaving home to find a new life and a new place to live where no one knew me or where I came from. Doing that would help me find the peace of mind I desperately needed. I was carrying a lot of guilt, carrying a crippling burden of shame across my shoulders. I needed to overcome some of that, and I needed to reach a point where I could forgive everyone, including myself, and I needed to do it before I lost myself forever.

I left Chicago and set out on a mission to improve my living conditions for myself and the children I took with me, four of someone else's and mine. I needed peace of mind and to be able to think and stop running. I'd wanted to learn from the people I grew up with, but it was too late for me to interview all the women of Bronzeville. They were all gone except for my mother and another woman who was a member of a family of crime figures.

The most notable member of her family was her brother. She had four brothers, and she was the only girl. Not one of them stood more than four feet five inches tall, but they walked tall as though they carried a big stick and weren't afraid of anyone.

One of her brothers was a handsome man, bowlegged, and charismatic; he was as fine as he could be. I had a mean crush on him and flirted with him often. He didn't take nothing from anyone. They all died at early ages of heart attacks, except for the sister. I heard from a friend that she is still living and just came home from the penitentiary.

Even so, most of the friends I grew up were gone too, so there is a compelling need for me to tell their stories—to tell their stories, to help put these kinds of life's experiences into perspective so that others who are caught up and can't seem to find their way out would know they are not alone and there is hope. I can't forget that they lived and how they suffered. I feel their lives should count for something—after all the mistakes they made, they were human beings, and they lived here on this earth. If their life stories can help someone to stay away from drugs, then that will be something they left behind worthwhile on this earth. They will have built an unknowing legacy for others to remember and to learn from them. I attribute my life to them because, if I had not seen what was happening to them, I might have fallen; in a sense, they saved my life. I was not any better than them. I feel they died so I might live, and maybe writing this book is supposed to happen for me and for them. I need to remember them often, and to do that, I had to make something of myself in honor of them. There must be justification for what happened to them; otherwise, their lives will be practically meaningless, and that is not okay. Every life has meaning. I remember them telling me not to never try drugs, telling me how awful it was, yet they had no control over it themselves. They may have said "Don't ever do it," but their lives were not a living testimony to their witness.

All the time, my heart was breaking for them. I tried so hard to help and encourage them to stop, but that is not the way it works with drugs. Drugs are stronger than any one person; the drugs were stronger than they were. I don't think I have ever heard a person addicted to a drug say they didn't love the high but they hated the pain of withdrawal that followed the high. To watch a heroin addict, go through withdrawal—that was almost unbearable; to watch a teenager endure such pain is unthinkable. I had to watch it every day. I felt so helpless that I could not do anything to help.

I saw my brother beat his head against a brick wall because he was in so much pain and needed a fix when he was locked up. I cried because there was nothing I could do for him other than give him a fix, and that could not happen. When the women of Bronzeville found out their children were using, they were sickened. They were strong, powerful women, but even they could not stand to see their children go through such pain. They did the parent thing and tried to get them to go to treatment. For others, if treatment failed, they cut them off until they could get them to go again. Then they sent them through treatment again.

It was not enough; the majority of them were not strong enough to stay away from the drugs, which was typical of heroin addicts. More often than not, they went back to using. There was something about heroin that no one seemed to be able to stay away from it. It is my sad, hard-earned knowledge that, if anyone says they can handle it, they will forever be a drug addict. No one can control drug addiction, and once you are an addict—even if you are recovering—you are still an addict. I get sick when I think about the opportunities in life my friends and family did not have and the pain they lived through in such a short period. None of this should have happened, not to anyone—poor, rich, White, or Black.

This is what happened in our lives. Children with no money are forced to live with the evils in this world, unlike the people who bring it into our communities. At the time I was growing up, Black people did not own ships or airplanes, but drugs seemed to find their way into the Black communities. I guess we were expendable. I would sit and think about what the people who brought it in thought about their families. Did they really think drugs would never touch their children? Over the years, I watched more and more suburban children become addicted to the same drugs the inner-city children were addicted to. It is the same as the women of Bronzeville's children; it touched them too. They never thought that the drugs they dealt to the others would trap their own children. How could they have? If they did, they wouldn't have done it. Like a thief in the Bible's night, it did.

My promise to myself was to not do it, and as my tribute to them, I would always remember them. I would also work to keep others away from drugs by telling the stories of all the women in Bronzeville, in hopes of saving as many I can. It has never been easy; life has a way of pulling you down, and it's up to you to get up and move out.

I was lucky to survive and come through it, though not until I dealt with my own issues. I knew they were harmful, and I didn't love them. I hated them for what they could do; I was afraid of them. I can't watch movies like *American Gangster*. Movies like those sicken me, and I find myself afraid that those may happen to me. I don't want anyone around me using drugs, and I need to keep my pledge to my friends and family.

I needed to remember the things that happened, even though it is difficult and at times unbearable to remember. I wanted to keep those promises to them, but to do that, I needed to begin with an understanding of our mothers and what they were thinking.

The 1980s

Death and Destruction

In 1981, my brother was murdered, shot in the back six times by a police officer. My mother came back to console us and grieve with us. Even though she was there, she wasn't there for me the way I thought she should have been, and once again I was supposed to be strong in the face of another tragedy in our life.

More than at any other time in my life, I knew it was time for me to go. It took me six months to prepare, but then my brother was murdered, and six months after that, I was assaulted by my stepfather's son.

My ten-year-old son was sleeping in the next room. I could hear him fighting to get away, and there was nothing I could do. I heard the back door slam and footsteps running after him. I was sure they had caught him and done something to him. I thought they caught him, but a while after, I heard the footsteps of the police and the ambulance coming up the stairs, and I knew he was all right. He had gone to a neighbor's house and called the police. I still couldn't move and couldn't see. I was taken to the hospital. I thought I had a black eye, and my face was swollen beyond recognition; it was much more severe than I could have ever imagined. I was in trouble and in so much pain.

I lay there in the emergency room for hours, trying to stay very still, careful to not stir the pain; somehow, my hand was cut and had to be stitched up. I was in so much pain, yet they couldn't give me pain medication because there was so much swelling that they could not assess the extent of the damage. They knew it was possible I could strangle on my own saliva or blood. I was strapped to a bed, sitting up for weeks until the swelling went down enough to do MRIs to assess the damage.

Once the MRI was complete, they found out every bone in my face was broken, including my nose, in fourteen places; the eye bone was broken, the facial nerve damaged, the floor of the orbit destroyed, sinus cavity gone. My eye was literally in my jaw, the lid had a ptosis and could not open, and the muscles were damaged. It would take multiple surgeries; even then there was no guarantee of my complete recovery. I didn't know why I sat in the emergency room so long without medication. My mother was by my side the entire time, fussing about my not getting pain medication.

They soon explained that my injuries were so extensive and so severe they couldn't medicate me and didn't want me to go to sleep because I could choke to death on my own saliva. My sinuses were gone, and I had what was called an orbital blowout fracture.

When I was placed in a room, I was told that I was in a very serious condition; they would not know just how serious until the swelling went down. In the meantime, I would remain in the hospital for some time. I never would have imagined how long I would have to be there, but it was a very long time.

The swelling went down some in about three weeks, and MRIs were done and CT scans were done. They found that my eye was down in my face, the floor of my orbit was no longer there, and the eye nerve was damaged. The eye bone was broken, my nose was broken in fourteen places, and the pupil in my eye was damaged and larger than the that of the other eye. I was told there wasn't much to be done about the eye or repairing the eye bone.

They said I was going to be blind for the rest of my life in the left eye.

I was not going to hear of that! I told the doctor that she didn't know me that well to say that to me, and I walked out of her office. I believed I would see again; not for one moment did I believe I would be blind in one eye. That was how strong my faith was and has always been. That comes from the foundation in the church and the foundation my family provided us in teaching us and keeping us in the church.

My mother and grandmothers had unshakable faith, something young people don't have today. I was told I would need several surgeries to repair the bones, but the worst part of this was to sleep sitting up, strapped to the bed for several weeks, knowing I could drown in my own blood. My facial cavities were fractured, and because of that, blood had no place to drain until tubes were put in.

I remained in the hospital for several weeks, had several surgeries: one to repair the bone damage and another to repair the eye bone and thread the nerve back through it. The nerve that controlled feeling in the face had been disturbed, and I no longer had feeling on the left side of my face. The doctors were unclear after the surgeries if the feeling would come back; there was no guarantee if the feeling would come back or that I would ever see out of that eye again.

I didn't believe anything they said. My life went right back to the teachings of my grandmothers and having to go to church every Sunday and my mother, her bible, and the insurmountable faith she had. This was the time that my faith was being tested. I had lost my brother six months earlier to a violent death, and I had not had enough time to mourn or grieve his death before my life was flashing before me! What a traumatic experience this was. It was the way things had always happened to others, not to me because I was always careful.

Living with Stress and Anxiety

Everything in my life was now in question. The stress was enormous.

The anxiety attacks were nearly unbearable, and every surgery I had made it that much more unbearable. Every time I went under the knife and under anesthesia, I thought I would not survive. The more I went under the anesthesia, the harder it was on my body and to recover from it.

The anxiety became worse no matter how strong I tried to be.

After the initial repair of the bones in my face, the orthopedic and plastic surgeon said they could do no more. I still had a ptosis of the upper lid, which meant my eyelid no longer had muscles to lift it; it stayed closed. The eye was still down in my face, there was still no place for my eye to sit, and the floor of the orbit in the eye socket was destroyed.

I was referred from Michael Reese Hospital to the University of Chicago hospitals, where I saw another surgeon. I was told that no one had been able to repair an injury such as mine or get the lid up; however, a young surgeon, twenty-six years old, would be willing to experiment with some treatments if I was willing to allow him to. I agreed; no one had a better idea.

His first experiment was to try to put in a plate under the eye for it to sit on, but that proved to be more difficult than I had imagined. I had to undergo several surgeries awake so they could align the left eye with the right eye so I wouldn't have double vision in the straight-ahead gaze. It was certain I was going to have double vision in every direction, but the doctors were determined to line up both eyes. I wouldn't have double vision in the straight-ahead gaze. What was so difficult about these surgeries was they had to move all the nerves under the eye to get the plate in and move the nerves back in place.

That was so much more painful; it was an almost-unbearable pain after each surgery. I could not move for days, afraid that, if I did, the pain would get worse. No medicine helped, not even morphine. The pain just would not stop.

It took several surgeries to align the left eye with the right eye, and when they were finally successful, I nearly wept with relief. I don't think I could have lived through much more. But now that that was repaired, it was time to work on the lid.

The young surgeon tried several different techniques, such as putting in a sling and attaching the lid to my skull over the eyebrow. That didn't work. He tried several other things, to no avail. He then decided to cut out the loose skin in the lid and sew the lid up. The lid then stayed up but would not close, and that is the way I would have to live for the rest of my life.

My eyelid always stays open, and I wear a patch over it at night to keep debris out and moisture in. I still had worries about dry eyes during the day, as well as worry about something flying into the eye. I would have to use eye drops several times a day and wear safety glasses when out, but I wouldn't look disfigured. Hopefully, no one would notice, but I knew, every time I looked in the mirror, I could see that I was disfigured. Even so, I was happy with what the doctors had done. Now when I look in the mirror, I see a very strong individual, one who will take no mess but who has compassion for everyone who will stand her ground, walk away if necessary, be the best she can be, choose her battles, change what she can change and not worry about the rest, pray for who needs praying for, and let go and let God do the rest. By the end of it all, I had had thirty-two surgeries over five years, and I was ready to go. It did not matter to me that I wasn't completely done with the surgeries. I would have to have regular surgeries to cut out scar tissue from time to time, probably for the rest of my life.

After the surgeries, the fear and anxiety became worse. I couldn't drive a car or ride the bus. Any noise I heard made me jump. I put bars on the doors and the windows, and I only went out if I had to go to work. The anxiety attacks got worse to the point I could not breathe and my throat would freeze. I couldn't swallow. I would have an anxiety attack, and the only thing that would help me was to run. I ran anytime but mostly in the middle of the night. The doctors connected me to a heart monitor, which was connected to the telephone every time it went off; they sent an ambulance to get me. My anxiety attacks were bad. My throat would freeze; my left side would become numb. I thought I was going to die. I thought the devil was coming to get me. I was depressed; my adrenaline would increase and make the symptom that much worse, but somehow, I still functioned enough to go to work every day. I eventually went to receive therapy and biofeedback for some time.

I read a book called *Hope and Help for Your Nerves* by Claire Weekes, which helped me to understand the nervous system and how and why I was having such severe anxiety attacks. I finally realized that I wasn't going to die at the onset of the anxiety attack, and much more to the point, it helped me to understand the nervous system and what happens when there are shocks to it and how the body reacts to compensate for those shocks.

That was the first step to the healing process for me although the anxiety never goes away. Now that I learned how to better control it, I have been able to think about the future.

I was on the way to healing, but I was set back once again. My mother and her misplaced priorities were in the way again. She was there by my side the whole time I was going through the surgeries, but when I was out of the hospital, her attentions turned to my perpetrator. He was her husband's son by another woman; he was, characteristically, raised by her and then by me after she went to the penitentiary.

His real mother decided she didn't want the baby boy she bore, and my mother her good and kind heart went to the hospital and got him, even though she had just had a baby a few months prior. I don't know why she took him in; maybe she was guilty because her baby was not her husband's either, or could it have been characteristically what Black women did? If we look back at slavery, when slaves were sold off from their children, the remaining slaves took them in and raised them as their own. It was what the women of Bronzeville did all the time. You be the judge.

Despite the horror of his attack, my mother protected him from going to the penitentiary. She minimized what he did to me. She minimized the hurt I felt and the emotional roller coaster I was on after he attacked me! I had so much rage in me for her that I literally believed the devil was coming to get me! Seemingly endless years of surgeries, all of them painful, and every one of them leaving me suffering, led only to the doctors declaring me legally blind. I then knew I had to leave Chicago.

Leaving Chicago, Determined to Succeed

My brother and his wife were taking care of the kids while I was incapacitated during recovery. Gangs were trying to recruit my children. They were getting into trouble and as full of anger at what had happened to me. But they took it out on their uncle, my brother. I needed to give them a better life than I had.

I needed to show them I was not going to allow the gangs to have them.

They needed to see that I was stronger than any gang and that I was determined they were not going to have my children.

I lived in regret, knowing I should have gone when I had a mind to after she came home and put me out. Finally, after the surgeries, the pain, and still living in the result of my upbringing, I got up the courage to pack up our bags put them in the car. It was me and five children. We took off driving in search of a new home. My stepson's mother was dying of a brain tumor. I didn't know that at that time. She must have known and unselfishly allowed him to leave with us to get him out of Chicago. He is now working, married, raised four children, and has been on his job for more than sixteen years. Another graduated high school and returned to Chicago and is a chef. The only girl graduated returned to Chicago and is now a working as an EMT. One died of leukemia in 2005. My son graduated and went on to earn a carpentry certificate.

The six of us left in search of a new life, not knowing where we were going or where we were going to live. I had taken down my pension for the university where I had worked for fifteen years and attended school. My pension is what is what we would live on until I found a job.

While I was idle and looking for work, I went to a trade school in Minneapolis and studied computer operations for five months. I then attended a university in Minnesota, taking one class at a time and almost seven years to complete an undergraduate bachelor's degree. It took so long because I needed to build on my reading, writing, and comprehension skills, and it took at least two years to do so. I also was raising these five children and had to see to it they received an education as well. I continued to complete a master's degree in education, cultural studies, writing/African American English with a minor in linguistics. I went to work as an adjunct professor at a different local university, teaching a class, Diversity in Education. I took out student loans to finish my education; it wasn't easy, but it was worth it, learning study habits in between parenting, working full-time. and attending school. Attending school events for the children and trying to keep them on track were a huge undertaking, but I needed to set an example for all of them.

I had to leave my extended family behind to find myself. I needed to feel safe for once in my life. I needed to have the same sense of safety that I'd felt before I was seven years old. I'd not felt that since we lived with my maternal grandmother in the South or with my paternal grandmother on the South Side of Chicago.

I needed for the children I was raising to feel safe as well. We all needed to have a life to look forward to. Even so, I would need to go back someday and work through all the bad things that happened to me. But before that, I needed to learn a new way of living without lying, manipulating, and scheming.

I needed to break free of the past and start a new future.

Fleeing west, we went through Milwaukee, but I didn't like too much industrial areas. We kept going and slowed down long enough for me to realize I didn't care for St. Paul, either. Only a little bit farther though, and we reached Minneapolis. It seemed all right, but

I was pretty sure I wasn't done. It didn't feel quite far enough from Chicago. I figured we'd settle briefly—well, long enough to go to back to school to get a master's degree in education and to raise the children and get them through school.

When they were safely grown, I could return to Chicago.

I found myself a therapist as well and then found a doctor to finish the surgeries.

When we settled in Minneapolis, I was at a point I could finally feel safe and do some of the things I set out to do. I wanted these children to grow up with the confidence needed to be successful. It was hard enough working through my feelings of loss.

Flashbacks

After I left, those feelings were still there flashing before me. I hated all of what I had experienced in my life. I was still angry and became even angrier about it. It seemed that there was nowhere for me to go to get away from it all. I was locked in the same hell I had let everyone else in. I could do nothing but watch them suffer. I don't think anyone could imagine the hurt I felt, the anger I felt because my mother had moved us from Mississippi, where we never encountered anything like this. Everyone had morals and principles there. My mother would never have come to this down South. My grandparents and my great-grandparents would not have stood for it. They were moral, God-fearing, proud people. There were times that I wished we had never migrated north. All I could think about was I didn't care if Jim Crow was hard in the South; it couldn't be as bad as what we had encountering here in the North!

Here, we were always wondering where the next meal would come from or whether we would have a roof over our heads. We would never have been subjected to the things we saw down South. We would never have been left alone.

Why did they teach us respect, morals, and principle and make us go to church every Sunday only to allow us to fall into this kind of despair? They would have never stood by and let my brother and my best friend become heroin addicts in the South.

I'd felt like I'd been thrown into this environment of chaos after living such a simple life a block up the street. Instead, I stood in the dirt and looked around me at the vacant lots, abandoned cars, empty buildings, and nodding junkies, all around me, and at seven years old, I asked God why he had done this to us. I wanted to know why people couldn't see what was happening to us and why no one was coming to our rescue.

My Brother Jeffro's Death in the '80s

Both my brothers went to jail and did two years, and after they came home, there was nothing for them; they needed a change from the same old drudgery of the neighborhood. One went back to the ugliness of using and doing what he did until he caught another case and was forced to go to treatment by a judge. The other became a wanderer and left Chicago; no one would see him again for several years, not until after our other brother was killed.

The judge made him go to Gateway Alcohol and Drug Treatment Center in Lake Villa, Illinois. It looked like things were going to get better for him. Even so, I couldn't shake that same premonition I'd had of him since he was thirteen, dead in his thirties.

I pushed that down and away; that is the only way I could get on with living. My mother was in the penitentiary, and I kept the kids together. Some relatives wanted to split them up, but I knew they would have been treated differently because no one wanted to take them in the first place. I certainly was not going to live with any of them. I could take care of myself. I was streetwise and knew how to survive. We were looked down on for a long time because we were poor and living in the ghetto. People felt like they were doing us a favor—a special favor. It was always implied that we would "owe them."

It was different when my mother was making money.

Some bought houses, and their children went to schools that she helped pay for, some of them got out of trouble, and she paid their legal fees. Yet we were the "bad children," and they didn't want their children around us.

My brother was deeply sensitive to this, but it seemed to me that he wasn't much for this world. I could see the pain in his eyes, and I could see death in his face. I knew long before he passed away that he would die at a young age. I could sense it. I could feel his death.

There was a time he overdosed; he came to the house to take a shower and change his clothes. He went upstairs to the bathroom and ran water as though he really were going to take a shower, but he was in there too long. Suddenly I heard this loud thump on the floor, and I ran to the bathroom door, but it was locked. I knocked and I knocked; he never answered. I ran back downstairs to get a knife to try to pry the door and unlock it. As I entered the bathroom, I saw my brother lying on the floor with the needle sticking out of his arm, I knew then he had overdosed. I was in a daze, running around in circles, trying to figure out what to do. I ran down to the kitchen to get some salt and water to shoot him up with. I had seen it done many, many times by other junkies when someone had overdosed. I watched my friends do it to friends and watched our mothers do it to junkies and junkies do it to themselves, so I figured it was worth the chance.

It couldn't have made things worse, and I was scared to death.

I did it. I shot the saltwater mix into his vein, got him up to his feet, and started walking him around outside and slapping him in the face.

That day was the most frightening day of my life. I don't care how many times I had seen it done; it was still as scary and as disgusting as it ever was.

When he came around, I told him he couldn't come back. If he did, I would have to search him to make sure he had nothing on him. I told him that this wouldn't ever happen again. Those words hurt me more than anything, because I was talking to my brother, whom I loved with all my heart. I think having to do this to my brother who has always been my protector and my best friend was the hardest thing I had ever had to do, but I couldn't go through that ever again.

Where we lived, you didn't call the police or the ambulance; you were always taught not to do that. It was an unspoken, unwritten code in the neighborhood because the police were not to be trusted. Every time the police were called, someone got hurt or died. My brother was a habitual drug user, and after that incident, he was arrested and did two years in jail at Statesville. It was after that that he went to Gateway. He stayed for at least three years. It was the best thing that had ever happened to him; it was a beautiful place, and the program was excellent. They took their clients back to their childhood, rebuilding values, morals, and principles in them, as well as working to create respect for themselves and others.

My brother was clean for many years while he worked as a drug counselor for a time, had a baby, and was living with his girlfriend. His son was four months old when the premonition I'd had when I was thirteen exploded into my life.

I woke up on April 2, 1981. It was just barely warmer than freezing, and it was supposed to be nicer later in the day. I got ready for work as I did every other day, and a sense of foreboding came over me. I couldn't shake it. All day long, I had this terrible feeling that brought fear and anxiety. I somehow knew something was wrong just as I did the day I was assaulted. Immediately my thoughts went to my brother. I called his girlfriend. She said he was gone and she hadn't seen him all morning. I asked her to have him call me when he got home, but that call never came.

Midday, I called him again, and she still had not seen him; even she was starting to worry.

What we didn't know was that my brother was socializing with a friend.

I got frantic, calling everyone I knew, but no one had seen him recently; he and his best friend were together.

At four o'clock that afternoon, I became even more anxious and then calm at the same time. For whatever reason, I knew he was gone. At the same time, I told myself that it couldn't be true. I tried wishing it not to be so, but deep in my heart, I knew he was gone.

I kept calling around anyway, searching for him. I went home from work and couldn't do anything but sit on the side of the bed and look at the wall for the rest of the day, waiting for the phone to ring. I couldn't move. I sat there on the side of the bed, eventually lying down, waiting, watching the clock.

At two o'clock in the morning, the phone rang. I looked at the phone for a second, knowing what was going to happen if I answered. But I had no choice. I had to know.

I picked up the phone.

It was my father. He said he was at the morgue and had identified my brother's body. I started weeping the moment I put the receiver to my head. The tears streamed down my face as I sat there on the side of the bed, unable to move. The only thing on my mind was *Lord, what am I going to do now?* My father said that they didn't know the circumstances surrounding the incident, only that he was shot in the back six times by an off-duty police officer. They had both been drinking at the bar. My brother died at 4:00 p.m., exactly the time I knew he was gone, dead of gunshot wounds to the back and side of the neck.

That was the time that I'd stopped calling around and looking for him because I knew he was gone; it was just confirmed that he died at 4:00 p.m.

Thankfully, there were witnesses to ensure that the off-duty Chicago police officer would never get away with it. No one knew anything else at the time. No one could explain why my brother was moving away from the off-duty officer or what the officer was doing with his gun drawn. But I know it is wrong to shoot someone in the back six times.

I don't remember who told my mother. I was the one who told my brothers and sisters. The next few days were the worst, planning his funeral services with my mother. I could see the hurt in her eyes, though she didn't shed a tear, showing true strength for her family. But I also knew she felt guilt about his death, and while she never let on, I knew it as surely as I knew my brother was to die in his thirties.

I am my mother's daughter, but I am not my mother. I cried every day. She comforted me, telling me, "He's gone now, honey, and you can't bring him back with tears."

A week later, we buried him.

On the day of his funeral, I walked into the parlor to find him in a casket that was fully opened head to toe. I had never seen that before. As far as I knew, no one opened a casket all the way.

He wore a gold medallion around his neck, over a brown suit, wearing brown shoes to match. The hardest thing in my life was seeing him lying in that casket. Music floated around us, the notes and words of "It's So Hard to Say Goodbye to Yesterday," an R & B song written by Motown husband-and-wife songwriting team Freddie Perren and Christine Yarian for the film *Cooley High* and performed by Motown artist G. C. Cameron.

For years after the funeral, I couldn't stand to hear that song; every time it played on the radio, I turned to another station.

We returned from my brother's funeral on April 9, 1981, only to find out that our next-door neighbor and friend had also been shot dead by a police officer, shot in the back three times. He'd been shopping in downtown Chicago and was supposed to have stolen a watch. He'd worked up the street from where we lived, at the neighborhood shoe store, and it turned out he had not stolen anything, just walking while Black, just like today in the age of Black Lives Matter, when so many Black young men are being gunned down in 2015. It is nothing new; it has been happening for many years. This young man was a wonderful young man, independent, a hard worker, and good student. We attended the same high school, Du Sable High School. I am not sure why he was gunned down, but it seems so senseless to me. I didn't attend his funeral; I couldn't stand it anymore. It wasn't long after that two more boys were killed in our neighborhood that I knew another was shot in the arm and left to bleed to death from a gunshot wound inflicted by the police, and because they did not get him help soon enough, he died of his wounds. The other was murdered by an unknown assailant. They had both been friends of mine and my brothers. This was all too common in our neighborhood in the 1950s, 1960s, and 1970s—Black boys being killed shot in the back.

There hasn't been a day in my life that I haven't thought about all the young people who died in my neighborhood. As Gwendolyn Brooks referred to in her book *A Street in Bronzeville*, "the boy died in my alley." I grew up in that same neighborhood. My experience in Bronzeville mirrored hers. I knew many boys who died in the alley where I lived.

Though my brother was gone, I knew it wasn't going to be the end of drug use in our family. That was all I wanted—for my family to be done with drugs. I knew my brother's death wouldn't be the only one. It was so hard because he was the one who broke the mold in our family; he was the first to die in five generations, but it was just a matter of time.

I would live the rest of my life counting the days, waiting for the next drug-related death. Was I paranoid? You bet I was, but I was also being realistic. I knew there were three endings to the story for someone using drugs: die from an overdose, rot most of their life away in jail, or completely turn their life around and move on.

Post-traumatic Stress Disorder (PTSD)

Post-traumatic stress disorder, or PTSD, I am told, is an anxiety disorder that stems from psychological trauma or a life-threatening event that occurred in your life. It can show up in feelings of unreasonable anger, being constantly edgy, intense flashbacks, nightmares, and the like.

I had PTSD and was afraid of everything and everyone. I would jump at my own shadow. No one had to tell me that I had PTSD. I didn't need to see a psychologist to know because I often wondered why I was still living. I thought I was going to die, too, just as so many before me had. I thought it was just a matter of time. Either that or I felt I would kill someone, protecting myself. The anger and anxiety I lived with were more than I could bear. I worried about everyone and everything. I was so afraid of living, thinking I would die. I was living in anticipation of my own death.

I knew the signs, and I also knew that something was going to happen to me if I didn't get out soon. I saw that just as I had seen my brother's death. I could feel the urgency of the necessity for my flight every day. I tried to get out. I tried to save something out of every paycheck so I could leave, but it always felt as if it were too little, too late or not enough. I didn't get out soon enough. As mentioned earlier, six months after my brother's death, I was assaulted in my bed while sleeping. In spite of it all, I survived and live to tell my story.

I am a walking miracle, and only the handiwork of God could have brought me through all this. My complete family upbringing gave me strength and determination against all odds.

Language and Culture, Strength and Determination

I was an African American English speaker (Creole speaker). I knew I had to learn to speak Standard American English. This was essential if I were going to be successful in my quest for an education. I had always been ridiculed in school because of how I talked, but I also knew that the way I spoke didn't just fall out of the sky and hit me in the head. I'd learned to speak this way from somewhere; I was not ignorant as some people claimed. The language of my family and my neighborhood had to originate from someplace.

I was determined to find where that place was. This was my incentive for returning to school. I had a need to know my heritage and my culture and the language I spoke that had always been marked as inferior to others. I had a need to prove to myself that I was not dumb and could be anything I wanted to be! So what if I was getting older than most college students were?

I didn't want to live in this world and not contribute something to it. I wanted to be remembered for something. I didn't want to die like all the others did. I wanted the world to know about the friends and family I lost who'd died. None of them had a chance to be all that they could be. I wanted them to live through me. I wanted to become their voice, the only voice they would ever have to speak to today about them to remember them and speak into the future.

I didn't want someone to say "Oh well, she lived, she died and left nothing to show that she ever lived." I did not want my life or their lives to account for nothing; they were special too, and they were special to me.

I returned to school eighteen years after I left, with a determination and a drive I didn't know I had in me. I was tired of people telling me I spoke incorrectly, that I didn't speak the King's English and, therefore, I would never go anywhere in the world.

They made me feel so ashamed of who I was and of my ancestors. After all, it was the way my people spoke, and I spoke like they did. I began to feel inadequate. I was confused about what was wrong with me and why I felt that way. I was determined that no one was going to make me feel that way ever again and was not going to deny my culture or heritage, nor was I going to assimilate White culture. I was going to be me and be proud. I was going to be Black and proud of it because the language I spoke had an origin, and I was going to find that origin.

I had never known there was a language called African American English or that it had a name. After returning to school, I was introduced to a professor who was a linguist. She introduced me to African American English, and I read many books on the subject. I met many professors of linguistics to help me learn about the language I spoke, where it came from, and how it evolved. As I read and learned, I remembered all the things my mother and grandmothers said. I was the kid who audiotaped everyone and had many tapes as far back as the 1960s of family reunions, a conversations of family members talking. They'd told me that education was empowerment. Then I knew why I went back to school: I was feeling empowered and validated for the first time in my educational life. I felt proud to be me. I was proud to be Black.

As I learned more about my culture and the men and women who had been slaves in my family, I began to respect the courage they had and what it took for them to endure the oppression they withstood for them to survive the mutilation and degradation served upon them during slavery. Because of them, I am here today. I feel as though I had inherited their strength. I didn't want to be shut out like I had been and felt so many years before in school. I was humiliated and treated with disrespect simply because of my culture, the way I spoke, and because of the color of my skin. I found out that I am 41 percent Nigerian, 22 percent European, 9 percent Native American, 12 percent Ivorian, the nationality of the ancestors who were the first slaves in my family.

Even so, I had to play the game once again to get back to school and then play the game to stay in school and survive.

I was in college, and college was where I would stay. As I studied and researched, I stumbled across hundreds of books and articles I never would have known existed. This was huge for me. It validated me and helped me recognize that I was not dumb. The way I spoke had a known origin, and I was not dumb because I spoke the way did. I now knew I could be myself and learn what I needed to learn and still be me. I could be proud of my ancestors, proud of being Black, and proud of the language of my people.

Of course, I was still angry that so much had been kept from me, but I didn't have to give up my culture to find it, and now I knew that I had two languages.

I knew I had to learn Standard English if I were going to be successful outside my community, but Black English was no longer a mark of inferiority to me. I could still have my culture, and I didn't have to be ashamed of who I was or deny my ancestors and the struggle they endured in slavery. Instead, I wanted to live up to the dignity and sacrifices they made so they would be proud of me. The fact that I could be educated and pay tribute to who they were set me free. It was apparent to me that culture and language are powerfully linked. As I furthered my education in the subject of Black English, I petitioned the university I was attending to allow me to declare African American English as my first language and American Standard English my second language, to study Black English in place of a second-language requirement. It had never been done before. It never occurred to me that my request would be denied.

Of course, they denied my request. I appealed their decision and appeared before the Scholastic Committee of English and Linguistics professors, prepared to explain to them why I thought they should allow me to study African American English in place of a second-language requirement. I gave them three reasons.

The first was that this language was part of my culture. I wanted to study it because I'd spent a lifetime ashamed of it, as if speaking it were a mark of feeblemindedness. I'd spent that same lifetime under a mandate to study White culture and White history.

Secondly, I was paying for my education and should be allowed to study anything I wanted to study as long as I studied it using prescribed methodology and practice.

Thirdly, my plan was to use this research to educate my own community as well as other educators because I knew that knowledge is powerful and teachers cannot teach what they don't know and kids would suffer as I did for that lack of knowledge.

After I addressed the committee, I, of course, had to wait. It should be clear by now that I am patient in some things but not necessarily in others. Even so, not long after, I received a letter in which they wrote, "You will be proud to know that this committee has decided to grant your request."

Stunned, I was then thrilled. Surely this has never been done before! I am certain that it has never been done since.

Language is, by far, the single most important tool in communicating within and between cultures. My goal for teachers was that they understand that, when teaching students of color, there is a need for teachers to take into account everyone's culture. My mission is to assure that every teacher understands that not every student who walks through the schoolroom door speaks, reads, writes, or understands Standard American English. Every school's curriculum should be culturally relevant, and the teachers must be culturally competent to successfully educate students of color.

Teachers need to know how to teach linguistically and culturally different children. That understanding is relevant to ensuring their success. The first step is to respect and understand the culture of the "other"; the second is that we educate and are aware of every student's culture and learning styles. We must know them to teach to their learning styles. Teachers must utilize prior student knowledge of their varied cultures and experiences of their students and allow students to bring their culture into the classroom. Allowing students to know they don't have to sacrifice their culture or who they are to be successful outside their community or in the classroom. On the other hand, the students must understand that they need to become bilingual to be successful in all settings. The community and the schools together can teach them self-efficacy skills and strategies. If this had happened for me, I might never have dropped out of school. Unfortunately, I grew up at a time when we didn't talk in the classroom about culture or the importance of having a culture. Growing up during a time when no one cared because students of color didn't really matter in the larger society.

In my opinion, the educational institutions need to understand that it is every student's right to a fair and equal education and a multicultural education under the laws of the Civil Rights Act. This will ensure that students will learn about one another and will have a better understanding of each culture and each culture's contribution to this country's wealth. If this does not occur, we will still have a continually widening achievement gap.

If we do not do this, we will have a continual decline in students of color enrolled in the higher-education institutions, and this country will suffer because of it.

The 1990s

Relationships

I had always had to be strong. It was expected of me, to not cry and to take charge and be in control. After my grandmother died, I was the caretaker in my family, raising my siblings. Even before that, before my grandmother moved in with us, I was the caregiver on occasions when my mother was gone for weeks at a time.

I was the one who worried about her. I had never had anyone show me the kind of care my grandmother did, and after she died, I had to hustle to get my mother home for the funeral with a matron and pay for the hotel for both and the airfare.

I had to learn to survive in the jungle. I learned to be manipulative, to steer my way through the chaos and mayhem, and I learned just enough to survive by playing the game instead of compromising my values and my principles.

I was confused. I didn't trust men or women. The only time I was ever able to have an intimate relationship was when I was sixteen, with a young man who was so understanding, patient with me. He was kind and thoughtful, and we dated for several years; it was the greatest relationship I have ever had in my life. He set the standard for the type of relationship I wanted to have a relationship with respect and compassion. He treated me in the way I wanted to be treated, with care and affection. He spoiled me for anyone else with gifts and movies and dinner out, walks through the park. And just as it began, it ended. He realized he was gay, and the relationship ended. We have kept in touch over the years and remained friends. As a result of my childhood experiences, I was never able to form intimate relationships with anyone since because I trusted no one, yet I was able to function in life and have distant relationships. I would not and could not show vulnerability to anyone. I could never let my guard down long enough to get caught up in true intimacy again.

During five years of surgeries, I cut my mother out of my life. I spoke to her occasionally by phone, but I was busy going to school and having surgeries.

After the move to Minneapolis, I still had to have several surgeries, but it was the move itself that drained me. I was away from family, I had no friends in my new home, and we all were incredibly lonely and homesick. I still had not dealt with my anxieties, I was still recovering from my surgeries, and I still had not dealt with my brother's death, never had time to grieve. I was still reliving the nightmare of the assault on me, and I had no idea how to begin to come to terms with my childhood experiences.

All these weighed heavily on me even while I was trying to raise healthy children who had already been exposed to so much life in the ghetto. All I wanted to do was to show them something different, a new way of living, and a new way of life. Moving was supposed to give us all a chance for a different and a better life.

Racism in the North

The move was to make things better; all it did was make them angry at me for taking them away from extended family and taking them to a predominantly White community. Minneapolis was a hotbed of racism that was so subtle and buried in the undercurrent that people refused to recognize its existence. They are just so guilty of it and in denial. People would say, "Minneapolis? There's no racism here! This is the North! We broke the slavery of the South!"

We all knew that was not true. The toughest kind of racism to fight against is the kind that is never acknowledged. Racism ignored, in which we go on with life and never acknowledge it, it will never go away. That is why it is the hardest to fight against.

It was tougher for my children here in the schools where there were, maybe, twenty African American students out of two thousand. The expectations for the African American students were low, and they weren't expected to succeed. My youngest boy was a United States Academic Achievement Award winner twice over, and he wasn't challenged enough in public schools. What he encountered in Minnesota schools turned him off completely to education. He was bored and felt as though he were being discriminated against because he was six feet tall at fourteen. I believe his White Minnesota classmates were afraid of him because he was so tall. They picked at him because his legs were too long to fit under the desk. Teachers and administrators sent me letters, saying he would not turn around and sit straight in his seat. I thought, *Are they crazy? His legs are too long to fit under the desk!* It wasn't just that; it was any little thing.

The move to Minnesota was supposed to change our lives for the better. If I had not made that decision to get out of Chicago, someone would have ended up dead. By moving, all of us were supposed to have a little more of a chance and take advantage of different opportunities. I certainly did not want to see another senseless death, but I was so angry that I knew, if I did not get out, it could have been me or them being killed. I thought, *What if I leave here and go there and one of them end up dying?* I knew for sure, if I did not leave there, one would for sure end up dying, so what choice did I have but to leave?

Acceptance of Kindness

I had been depressed enough and had enough fear for a lifetime. In the middle of me suffering from PTSD in Minneapolis, it was getting worse due to the stress of not having extended family and the kids' anger. The kids were rebelling; I was sick and had to have surgery unrelated to my eye. I felt alone, struggling to survive, and I had no one to turn to. The money I had left from taking down my pension plan from the university where I had worked for the last fifteen years was dwindling.

I had a part-time job working for the county, and I was attending school, and now all this was coming to an end again because I needed more surgery. I had several tumors in my back and stomach that were causing me a great deal of pain. I had severe anxiety and fears. I didn't know anyone, and I certainly had no idea what doctors to see.

I went to the phone book and ended up in an association in Uptown, Minneapolis. They referred me to another physician for women's health. I contacted them and made an appointment. The doctor I had the appointment with was a white woman in her midthirties. When I walked into her office, I immediately thought to myself, *She is gay.* I didn't know whether to stay or turn around and walk out. I didn't understand my feelings or why this was such a problem, because she was a doctor, and I needed a doctor right then.

I had been raised in a community where there were many people who were gay and were just a part of the community. My brother was gay, and I even dated a gay man, so why was I having such a hard time? Maybe it was bringing back memories of the old neighborhood and me running from and avoiding everything that I felt threatened by. As I walked into her office, I knew right away she was gay, yet I think my upbringing helped me to accept that and seek the help I needed. I was always taught to respect everyone and not stand in judgment of anyone.

As it turned out, she was kind, nurturing, caring, and I suppose she could see the fear in my eyes.

She became like a mother to me, someone I was missing in my life. She treated me with the kind of caring and nurturing a mother would give to a child. It was something I had missed and longed for in my life. After the surgery was over and I was getting healthy again, I went to her office for what was going to be last visit for me. She had given me hope, and I appreciated her for that. She gave me the support when I needed it most. I needed to get through a tough time at that moment.

At the time, it was so difficult to say goodbye because I had experienced something I had never experienced before. I wanted more, but she was not my mother; the life I grew up in had taken its toll on me. I really could not relate to anyone because I saw men abuse women so badly; I saw the prostitutes turning tricks with men who took advantage of them and treated them like animals. We watched women abuse themselves with drugs; pimps abused women and then became sweet to them and conned them after they got the money.

I hated what I saw and was so afraid of it at the same time. There was nowhere for me to run, and I wasn't trusting of anyone or anything. I was not allowing anyone to get close to me.

The 2000s

The Dialogue with Mama—It's Now or Never

I mentioned in an earlier chapter that, years after my mother returned from the penitentiary, I told her I was going to write about her life and the lives of the other women of Bronzeville, and her response was "No, you are not gone do no such a thang, honey! Them folks will kill you! Those people are powerful and dangerous people, and you don't mess with them." My mother was thinking I would tell all the dirty little secrets. I learned about the people she did business with, but she was more afraid of what I would say and who would be listening to what I had to say. She knew them all well. I responded to her strong warning of fear with my own conviction that I really needed to do this. I promised her, "I'm not going to use their names. I'm only going to tell about how I met them and your involvement in business connections with them. Besides, they're all gone, most of them. How much harm can I do?" She still contended strongly, "You don't know what they is capable of doing." She was right; they were dangerous, but they're all gone, and she still strongly voiced her opinion, "I don't care if most of them is gone or not! They have friends, and you don't know who is or how dangerous they are. I said back to her, "I have a story to tell about the profound impact they all had on my life." The misery they brought, what they did to me and my family; it changed my life in some ways for the better because since then I never wanted to live that way or have any connection to anyone connected to crime or drugs be a part of my life, ever again.

My mother would never discuss her business with me or her relationship with her other business partners. From the day she left the federal penitentiary at Alderson, West Virginia, in 1971, she never once discussed her life before or after. I always wanted to ask her questions about her life before and after she immigrated north to Chicago. I know my mother had a tough life in the South, living Jim Crow—who wasn't a real person, rather the name of the nineteenth-century minstrel song that had come to personify the effect of the system of government-sanctioned racial oppression and segregation in the United States that affected the lives of millions of African Americans! My mother's family members were sharecroppers in the South and lived Jim Crow. From rumors I heard growing up, sexual abuse had been part of that life as well. This is something no one wants to discuss, but I know it was something Black women experienced dating back to slavery. Today I say it is a part of the "post-traumatic slave syndrome" (term coined by Dr. Joy DeGrue), which still happens in the Black community. No one wants to talk about Black girls being robbed of their innocence. The questions I had for my mother and needed answers to were "Did you regret what you did? Do you regret what we went through and all the pain and the agony we suffered?"

I already knew the answer as to why she did what she did: I had concluded that she did for us. I wish she hadn't, and I just really wanted to hear it come out of her mouth if there were any regrets. I thought I deserved that much because I wanted to know that my mother had a heart and that we mattered in all of it.

Our relationship wasn't what it once was years ago. I felt for a very long time that I could not have asked her anything concerning her business. I may have gotten cursed out or told to mind my own business. It took a lot of nerve even now to ask, maybe because, after she returned home, we'd spent so much time apart, I didn't know where to start. I was still angry with her because she had to leave us. I never felt I had ever been allowed to be a child. I was always taking care of her children. Even when I was seven, I was rocking her babies.

We were estranged in later years, but after she came home, we lived in the same house for a short time. We were not that close—not like we were before she got into the business of selling drugs. Even so, I decided that it was now or never. This was the time to talk to her about this. It was the most important thing to me because it was the beginning of a new relationship for me and for her. This was the time because she wasn't getting any younger. She was eighty-five years old now. Who knows how much time we have left to get it right? I wanted this to happen before it was too late. I thought I would take this opportunity to question her. It was really, really important to me and for the rest of us to come to terms with everything we experienced as "children of the ghetto." I needed to clear the air once and for all. I needed to understand what she had to say. But there were no assurances that she'd say anything at all. She wasn't one to talk about her business or her life, especially to her children.

But we were no longer children. It was time for healing.

As Mary G. Blige's song goes, "Children of the ghetto, keep your head to the sky." That was a powerful song. I could identify with it because that is what we did: we kept our heads to the sky; we survived. We survived the ghetto, defied the odds, and cheated the statistics because, according to history, we were supposed to be statistics. I wanted to finally get some answers in her own words, from her own mouth. I probably already knew the answers, but hearing her speak would verify the facts and validate the truth. I was hurting inside even though I understood why she turned to a life of crime. I was totally displeased with her decision. Her life choices might have destroyed our lives, and I wanted to know if she understood the trauma we had suffered. I had questions bottled up inside for as long as I can remember, wondering, what if? What if things had been different? What if she had not done those things? What if we'd had a different upbringing? What if we had stayed in the south? Would we have turned out any differently?

I know I would have. My life would have been a lot easier, and I would not have blossomed so late in life. My relationships would have been different as well, and perhaps it may have been easier to bond with others. I might have been more trusting too.

The first question I asked my mother was how she felt about what she did and what they did. I wanted to know if she had any remorse or if she regretted any of it. All I've ever thought of is how I could have had a different life had it not been for what they did. I could also look on the other side—the good side of it. My life is not so bad now because of what I learned then, but I believe my life could have been better. When I finally asked my mother a question, she hesitated, as if she were preparing an answer. I said, "It's okay. We've all forgiven you. We've quietly come to terms with it, and I understand why you did what you did. You really wanted to give us a better chance in life. You were tired of seeing us go hungry and going without the things we needed."

To tell the truth, though, we all had residual effects from her life choices. Some of us were still trying to get a grip on life. We were struggling to live and make sense of all the bad things that we experienced and saw. We were struggling to make sure we weren't going to be products of our environment. I was trying hard to set a different kind of example for my siblings while she was away.

When my mother felt comfortable enough to answer, she said, "I sold many a bag a dope. I wasn't proud of what I had done." Then she stopped, gathered her thoughts again. "We were selling ten capsules for ten dollars, and then we was selling an eighth of an ounce for thirty dollars and from there to ounces. We were making money hand over fist in the beginning, and then we were paying the police." She stopped again because she was eighty-five years old and needed to think about what she was saying, but she didn't want to talk about it any longer, so she stopped there. She never really wanted to discuss her life. I don't know if she was ashamed of her past or if she just didn't want to talk about it with us. She was very private like that. The fact is that this was no small-time stuff. They did business with the Mafia itself, high-powered lawyers, and judges.

Despite whom they dealt with, I want people to know the good these women of Bronzeville did for their community. But I also want people to know the bad that came out of it. I want people to know about the many prominent citizens who otherwise went unnoticed while, at the same time, they were doing so much harm to so many, including themselves. I wanted people to understand the world I grew up in, a world so cruel that it would let God-fearing women who'd never done anything wrong in their whole lives become involved in a life of crime to survive and feed their children, the same way they, the heartless, took away the children of slaves and sold them off for their own well-being. The lives of crime of the prominent would put the women of Bronzeville and their children in situations so bad that they could find no other choice but to turn to the very same life of crime in their neighborhoods that helped to feed their own children. So many women today are at risk due to the same circumstances of poverty.

There is not much written about the experiences of Black women by Black women, about their experience during and after their immigration to the North. I haven't found much that discusses the experiences of Black women leaving their homes, their families, and their pearls. There seems to be nothing about what Black women faced while trying to survive in the North, especially after their men were forced out of their homes.

It is no wonder to me why men left their women and children. It is no mystery why the breakup of the Black family structure, which began in the Deep South, perpetuated through the years into the present. The rules, regulations, and laws both were against Black families—whom does it help? It only hinders and drives a wedge between family members and is just another way of keeping the poor down; it is designed that way. If you don't have a driver's license, how do you get to work? If you make minimum wage, how do you pay child support and maintain a way to get to work? That is why so many drive every day without a license or don't work at all. It's easy to see why the poor are unable to progress in life and feel the only way to live is by breaking laws set up against them.

The Day My Mother Died

My mother passed away on August 3, 2008, at the age of eighty-nine. I felt something was wrong that entire week, and I could not shake it. I called her every day that week twice a day, worried and fearful of my mother's death, just as I had felt the day my brother was killed. I was overtaken by the fear. I knew it was her time to go, just as I had known all the other deaths before her.

This fear I had was just as debilitating as it had been when I was growing up, when I worried so much and so hard for her safety. I'd known my sister, my brother, and my nephew whom I raised were all destined to die. I could see it; I could feel it. I can't tell you how I knew; I just did, and it was a lifetime of worry for each of them. The anticipation was even worse. That week, everything she ever told me or taught me flashed in and through my mind. How she taught me to overcome racism and not to hate in return, that the universe took care of everything and was the equalizer of all things. She educated me on how to survive and be the best person I could be in life, to live in the worst shit yet come out on the other side smelling like a rose. My mother always taught me that other people's hate was their problem and not mine and, if I took on that hate, it would become my problem, and hate destroys; don't allow it to destroy you. I grew up in a time when elders did the teachings, providing us with. "valuable race lessons, about the historical struggle of Black Americans against systemic racism and oppression" (Jackman and Carne 1986) My mother was adamant that I be literate about the subject of race relation and the political process, not just in experience but also in education. She educated me well about survival skills and, most importantly, common sense and vital lessons in common sense. As I thought about her that week, the fear of losing her created more anxiety than I was prepared to deal with at that moment.

When she called me that day to tell me she was alone, she sounded so afraid. I knew she needed to have someone with her. I tried to reassure her that I would take care of it and get someone over there immediately so she wouldn't be alone. My mother knew I would jump anytime she called and keep my word, even if I had to get on the highway and be there in six hours myself.

She knew I would get on the phone and call every family member until someone went over. I called my brother and told him to get over there. I told him that I thought it was urgent. I explained to him what I was feeling. I wouldn't take no for an answer. I called my mother back and told her he was on his way. I told her I was going to be there as soon as I could make arrangements to travel there. The brother next to my youngest brother went over there right away and spent the evening with her. Just before I said goodbye, I said to her, "Just hold on."

I really didn't mean to say that, but the feeling inside me was so urgent and telling me that it was her time to go. I just couldn't shake it. I knew it was going to happen. I felt it the way I always feel when death is lurking in the wings. All my life, I could feel those kinds of things, whenever death was creeping in. I don't know if it was because I had seen so much death or if it was a supernatural gift, but I wasn't the only one who experienced those feelings. My younger sister predicted her friend's death and another person's death. It happened just the way she saw it. My mother and my niece also could feel death.

I knew then that my mother knew it was her time to go. She'd called everyone she knew that week. The day before she left, she called her only living brother and talked with him for two hours. She also called my cousin, my niece, and told them she was all alone, and they, in turn, called me. She wasn't alone that day; her home health nurse was there with her, and my sister was there for part of the day. Maybe she wanted the rest of her family there with her too. I still believe she was trying to say goodbye.

My sister was going on vacation that day, and my mother told her, "I may not be here when you get back." She knew she was going. Why is it we never pay attention to those types of statements?

Everyone I know who has passed away has given some indication they were leaving. It's what my brother did just before he passed away. He said straight to me, "I am not going to make it. I would like for you to take care of my son." But I already knew my brother wasn't going to make it.

My nephew said the same thing in his letter before he passed. He said, "Mama, I will see you soon." No one paid any attention to that statement in his letter at that time. Then it came to mind after he passed away two weeks later, after my sister, his mother, passed away. He died at the age of thirty-five. There was no apparent reason, and he had never been sick a day in his life. I'd called my mother the day before and right after work because I was so worried it was on a Friday. By the time I left work, several family members were there, and she had a house full of company. My cousin was there with her grandchildren. She had visited my mother every week for years. My mother was like another mother to her, and she felt that my mother was just like a mother to her.

My brother was there for most of the evening, and we all talked with Mama before she went to bed. We'd done this by phone or in person every morning and every evening for a long time. My brother called her and spoke with her. He often teased her about being such a big baby, and she got a big chuckle out of that. My brothers put her to bed, and she went to sleep as she normally did. Still at home, I didn't sleep well that night. I just wanted her to hold on until I could get there.

But it wasn't to be. I woke up that Sunday morning, reaching for the phone to call her as I did every morning when I thought she would be awake. As my fingers touched the phone, it rang. I knew instantly that it was about my mother. No one in my family ever called me that time of morning because, as a rule of thumb, calls in the wee hours of the morning could only mean one thing: death or serious trouble. Late-night or early-morning phone calls brought bad news. Black people lived on the edge like that due to poverty, racist acts, and other violent acts. Fear is so universal that it always seems that we get bad-news calls late at night or early in the morning.

To this day, I dread more than anything else, late-night calls, absolutely not after 10:00 p.m. I will let anyone else who knows me not to call after 9:00 p.m. if they can at all help it, because it frightens me. I went to answer the phone with apprehension. My heart was pounding loud, like a tiny someone in my chest had a steady beat on a drum. I could feel the same pounding in my temples.

I picked up the phone, and the voice on the other end said, "Hello?"

It was my brother's voice as he said softly, "Mama died this morning."

"No!" I cried, nearly dropping the phone. I immediately went into a state of shock, repeating over and over, "No! No! No!" even though deep down inside me I knew it was true. There was nothing I could do about it, no matter how much I cried or how badly I felt. I hurt deep down in my soul. This was the final call. She was gone, and there was no bringing her back. I remembered her same words to me when my brother died. She said, "Honey, no need in crying, no amount of tears is going to bring him back." There was nothing to be done but to accept that it was done.

I was not there when she left, and maybe I was not supposed to be there. I did have a little guilt about not getting there in time, but I went to see her often, and I felt I had been the kind of daughter she trusted and loved. No matter what she had done, she knew I loved and appreciated her, and that helped me get through. I spent a lifetime trying to make my mother proud of me; she knew she could trust anything I said. Her proudest moment, I think, was when she came to Minnesota for my graduation from my master's program at the University of Minnesota. I had been a high school dropout, and she had always preached the importance of an education. I think that gave her a sense of pride and I felt that same pride.

I had been taught what the Bible says, "Honor thy father and thy mother." No matter what, the knowledge that I had gotten right with her was the reality that helped then and is helping me even today, to get through the pain and the hurt of losing her. What I knew then and know now deep in my heart is that I will always have her near; no matter what she had done, she was my mother, and I will always love her.

In my early years of life, my mother and I were estranged because of her lifestyle, and the many commonsense things she taught me negated some of the things she had done and said to me. I never understood why she accused me of messing with her men while, at the same time, she was propositioning me off to others who touched me inappropriately. She used me so that she could get what she wanted from them.

I knew that that was how she had been treated when she was young. I don't think she knew any better, and if she did, I needed for her to have an excuse to justify it. I did play the game with them—but when it came down to them touching me on my private parts, I drew the line. Working through my anger, working through to understanding, was what I had done ever since those days as a child and a teenager. But now she was gone, and I could lay her to rest—as well as my feelings.

I had expected her death, just as I had expected my brother's death so many years ago. It was the only thing in my life that I deeply and truly feared—not having my mother in my life. The fact that she was eighty-nine years old when she died had just made the fear more drawn out than anything else I had ever experienced, the anticipation of death.

My mother was a few months shy of making her ninetieth birthday, and with her death, she was the last woman of the women of Bronzeville—all her sisters in crime all passed on. We all thought she would make it to be one hundred years old because she was so strong, so strong-willed, and so wise—even despite her shortcomings. She'd not been sick to our knowledge, so that made it that much harder to come to terms with her sudden death. Yet everyone thought it was such a blessing that we didn't have to see her suffer or be sick for a long period.

She had family with her, and she was laughing and joking around, and when they'd all grown tired, she went to bed happy. I guess it was fitting for her to go the way she did; she died in her sleep.

Everything had to be on her own terms just as she had lived her life on her own terms. She said her goodbyes went to sleep and just slept on, hopefully, right into her next life. I know she won't remember me in her next life, but her sprit will look over all of us, and that is a profound comfort to me. How does one feel when you know you will never see someone you love ever again? It makes me wonder how my great-grandmother felt when her two children were sold off from her into slavery, never to be seen again? The feelings are indescribable.

Shortly after, I went home to Chicago to be with the rest of the family and to attend the funeral. I stayed at her house and lay in her bed every night, sleeping there the entire time I was there. It was comforting to me to lie where she had lain.

This woman's story is one of many about Black women who have not yet been told; that needs be told. I have not known a Black woman who has not lived a hard life in my entire life. Black women have never, to my knowledge, been protected or pampered by anyone, not even their men, except my brother's wife. Remember I said I haven't ever seen it. They have always done the pampering and the protecting of their men and children to save them from the master's wrath, forced to mother White women's children during slavery and to care for the children of other slaves who were sold off. Black women have never been appreciated for anything they have contributed to this society. I am sure there are a few exceptions somewhere. I just haven't had the pleasure of seeing that until today. I see my brothers treating their wives with respect and appreciation. I guess it came from what they were taught from our mother. Black women were forced to mother White people's children before their own, do anything the master forced them to do.

When I was young, during my mother's or my generation, growing up in Bronzeville, I never saw Black women treated very well. They were always abused and beaten, and if they were strong enough to advocate for themselves, they were alone. Some things are rare for Black women, like a smile. There was not a lot to smile about. There is a lot of sacrificing, hard work and childrearing, and trying to be inspiring to others. It's the role of the Black women in my life to be selfless. The Black women I knew were the matriarchs of the entire Black community, yet somehow, they never get the credit they deserve. It was important to me that I did everything I could to honor my mother and grandmothers because I know the sacrifices they made. I know what my mother suffered through in childhood. I know she wanted the best for all of us.

Everyone said we should be grateful that our mother passed on in her sleep.

I hate the word "died," even "passed away." It is so disagreeable to me. I have always preferred the words "left while she was sleeping" or "She slept on."

Everyone said they would prefer to go the way she went, but I would prefer she didn't go at all. It's still hard, even while knowing that it is a destiny we will all embark upon. I hope I will see her again. If I didn't think that way, I could not bear the sadness of losing her.

My mother's life toward the end had involved being bound by a wheelchair for twelve years as she'd had three strokes. She survived all three even though the doctors counted her out and told us she was going to die each time. Even when she survived, they said it was just a matter of time. I didn't feel she was going to go the first time; once again I had that feeling and was confident she would make it. I knew she wasn't going to die, and I told them so.

Her doctor asked me why I traveled up and down the highway every couple of days while she was in a coma. He said it was senseless. I said to him, "This is my mother! She knows I am here!"

Each one of her children was there at one time or another, taking turns staying with her. Someone was there twenty-four hours a day. She was never left alone, not for one minute, not for one hour, not for one day. I did not believe she was going to go. None of us did. That is how strong our faith was then and is now. I felt certain that my mother knew we were there.

Following each stroke, they told us the same thing! After the third stroke, she was in a coma for weeks. They told us to make preparations, and once again, they called a formal family meeting. It was standard protocol to tell us that she would likely go in her sleep.

We told them she was not going to die or we would have felt it, once again they didn't believe us. I think that doctors don't deal in faith that much, but they should have a little faith—at least a little spiritualism and hope because again they were wrong. She woke up, and finally, one of the doctors said, "There must be something to the kind of faith your family possesses. We've never seen anything like this before."

They seemed as certain that she was going to go just as they had been many years earlier that I was going to be blind for the rest of my life. I'd told them then they did not know what they were talking about, and they didn't. I knew they were wrong then, and I knew they were wrong once again with my mother. This is, once again, faith at work.

The third one was my mother's worst stroke. This time, she was left paralyzed on her left side and needed rehabilitation. She was so afraid of going to a nursing home. Like with most Black people, nursing homes are one of their worst nightmares. She feared how she might be treated. Like most Black people, we have little trust in places like these because of the historical way Black people have been treated and experimented on. She was afraid of being left alone there and of being mistreated. We reassured her that we would never allow that to happen to her, that one of us would be there night and day. When she finally agreed to a stay in a nursing home for rehabilitation, she was assured we would be there night and day. She had visitors twenty-four hours a day, and one of us spent the night with her until she came home. She was so right to be afraid; it was amazing how the people at the nursing home thought it was so strange for us to be so close to her. Even other residents said they couldn't believe so many people were in and out to see my mother every day! People from the old neighborhood, both young and old, all who appreciated my mother for what she had done for them, and there were people from out of town—nieces, nephews, cousins, siblings, and friends. She was the only Black woman at the rehab center. Does it make a difference that she was the only Black person there? It did because so often people leave their loved ones in homes and never visit because they don't want to take the time out of their busy lives. That was never something Black people did, though I can see that today it is becoming more common among us. My mother knew it because she worked in the nursing field after she came home from the penitentiary.

While she was there, Christmas came. For many of the other residents, there were no visitors. What a sad time, to not have visitors at Christmas. I couldn't believe that no one came to visit even on Christmas, so we shared our visits with them, ate with them, played games with them, held conversations with them. They were sad to see my mother leave because they enjoyed our company so much, and she was so proud of that.

She was so proud of us being there all the time and spending time with the other residents. There were many comments about our diligence in taking care of our mother. I think for the first time our mother knew we were never going to allow her to ever feel alone like the others did. She'd always been her own person and never vulnerable to anyone in her life. She never had to depend on anyone in her life. But once we nursed her through that last stroke, she was spoiled from then on! She was still the matriarch of this family, and we all knew it. My mother lived another eighteen years after her third stroke. We took her home to a new condo, where my sister Sandra moved from Washington, DC, to care for her, and from that day forward, she had twenty-four hours of care until the day she left.

To my mother's credit, she never told me anything in my life that didn't come to pass. She had great faith, great intuition, great determination, and she had more common sense than anyone I ever met. If she told me something about life, I could take it to the bank. She taught me to be responsible for my behavior and to stand up for what I believed in. When I did that, she made sure I knew that I would have to take the consequences for my actions just as she always did.

She taught me to listen and to learn, to take what was important to me in life, to learn from it and that I should take the misfortune of others and learn from that as well. She made sure I knew not to repeat the mistakes of others, as well as the mistakes she had made. I was never to blame someone else for the results of a poor choice on my part, nor was I allowed to pass judgment on anyone. Above everything else, I was to have respect for everyone, including myself and my elders. She said the elders were the ones with the wisdom that I will learn the most from. She taught me to always think for myself and that education is the best teacher and the best way out of poverty. She always said that, when you don't *listen* and you think you know it all, nothing can penetrate your brain; therefore, you can't learn anything. She taught me that you could always turn to God for salvation. She practiced that every day by reading her bible.

The day I got the call from my brother was the day I'd dreaded all my life. The words my brother spoke that faith-filled morning when he called to tell me my mother was gone were the most indescribable words I will ever hear in my lifetime ever again.

Ma Is What We Called Her

I never knew my paternal grandmother's maiden name. I knew she migrated north with my mother and father during the Great Migration, but that was about all I knew. That doesn't make me feel very good because I should know these things especially because she helped raise us and instilled in us moral character and core values. She protected us. Ma was instrumental in our lives from the beginning, and whatever successes we have had in our lives can be directly attributed to her. Ma posted the Ten Commandments on the refrigerator; you had to read them before you could go into the refrigerator. If you didn't go to church or to school, you didn't go out to play, watch TV, or do anything else. You didn't talk back to adults, roll your eyes, or pout your lips. You respected teachers, and you knew not to get a phone call home, or that was your behind. You ate dinner with the family every night and were in the house by the time the streetlights came on. There were rules and structure, unlike today, when children as young as kindergarten can say very disrespectful things to adults, and teachers and parents allow it. If it were me, I would get a backhand and would not dare utter a word whether right or wrong. Children were not allowed to participate in grown folks' business. You stayed in a child's place.

I knew very little about Ma when I was growing up, but she was Grandma. When I realized I didn't know very much about Ma, I did some digging and found a niece of hers who shared information with me. Ma's maiden name was Lois McCullum, and she was from Hattiesburg, Mississippi; that is the extent of what I know about her past, aside from the fact that she had five sisters and two brothers. Ma left Mississippi with my mother and father during the Great Migration.

My mother was the first to leave the South in her family, and later, three of her siblings followed her. My uncle was chased out of Mississippi by the Klan because he worked on the voters registration drive with a late, great civil rights leader. The story goes that my grandparents and my mother had to sneak him out of Jackson, Mississippi, in the dark of night just as the slaves had been moved through the Underground Railroad. If he had not left, he also would have been murdered just as the civil rights leader was murdered two weeks later. He and one of his sisters who escaped with him settled in Milwaukee, Wisconsin. An aunt migrated to Chicago, following my mother, and another settled in Minneapolis, Minnesota. The rest of my mother's siblings remained in the South.

My mother was the kind of person who would give her last dollar to anyone who asked, and then she'd sit down with her historical family bible—passed down from generation to generation with its dates: births, deaths, marriages, and anything else important, dating back to slavery. The Bible was where most black people kept important dates. She would pray that the Lord would help her make ends meet on that day. She never asked for too much or more than she needed. If there was a need for the next day, as there always was, she would get out that bible and pray some more, sing and hum some more. No matter what she had to do that day, telling stories of my mother's grandparents, who had been slaves, or doing a deal, she'd take the time to hold that bible and pray.

Sometimes I would be so mad at her because she had just given away our food money. I didn't know how we were going to eat, but she believed we would. That's how strong her faith was, and that is what she instilled in each of us: to always have unshakable faith. Even now, I find myself doing the same thing without worrying about how I will make ends meet. It took a long time to understand, but I think we all figured it out how strongly she believed. She passed to us that unshakable faith. On many occasions, she sat with that bible, humming and singing old slave songs and church hymns and praying. It should have been easy to dismiss, to let my anger blind me, but it seemed like her prayers would always be answered. Money seemed to fall out of the sky, or someone would knock on the door and say "Here's that two dollars I owe you from last time," and it was always at the right time. It never seemed to fail.

Years later, this is what my brother wrote about our mother:

> A very interesting woman my mother was. She never ceased to amaze me. She outlived a son and a daughter, two grandchildren, four husbands or life partners, eight siblings, and four women who were her partners in crime. My mother lived through the Depression, survived unbridled racism in the South, lived through segregation, and survived three years in a federal penitentiary. She conquered poverty and racial oppression in the North, raised a village, brought up devoted children with integrity, raised men to support their children and families, and taught women the importance of being educated and to think for themselves. She nurtured a prophet and a preacher, owned her own home and acres of land, which she worked for and inherited—land that had nothing to do with organized crime. She was the matriarch of an extensive family where what she said is what was done by all. She always had the last word.

Everyone did what she said out of respect for her. She had help from my grandmother, who was as strong as she was. My father's mother was there to support her and us. To make sure we had God in our lives, we attend church every Wednesday and Sunday.

My mother couldn't stand being poor. She couldn't stand weakness. If she thought you were weak, she felt that you needed taking care of and to be protected, she didn't respect you; she didn't respect weakness. Those she considered strong had to stand on their own

220

two feet. She wouldn't have it any other way. Once you stood on your own two feet, then and only then were you deserving of her respect. She endured heartache and physical pain every day of her life in later years but woke up every morning with a smile on her face. She touched the lives and feelings of countless others, gave to others at her own expense; she didn't play with God's sacraments. My mother lived a long time, long enough to be a downright pain in the you know what whenever she felt like it! She would laugh about it in her own mischievous little way, and she knew exactly how to play one of us against the other to achieve what she wanted.

One thing I remember most clearly was my experience in later years with her whenever I would go home for a visit. She would wake me up in the morning with a cup of hot chocolate and a breakfast tray with her homemade biscuits and bacon and eggs with some homemade stewed apples. She was a great cook; she had her mother's talents and recipes. Her cooking those foods for me was special. It was what I longed for from her when I was a little girl—like she did before, when I was seven years old. I missed that in the intervening years, but it was special when I became an adult. I'd also learned how to appreciate it more. What we can all say about her is she lived her life her way!

To me it seems that respect is no longer what is happening in this country. We have an African American president, and he gets no respect from his colleagues. They refer to him as Obama, not President Obama or Mr. President. It seems like racism is alive and well, and that has not much changed since the 1950s. You would think that from the time I was born, in 1946, to today, in 2015, things would have changed tremendously. But it has not. Race in America is still an issue and is still "America in black and white."

I have followed my mother's teaching when it comes to being politically savvy and have kept tabs on each political party for years. Having lived to see twelve presidents in my lifetime, I agree with my mother's point of view. She was very wise when she continually stressed the importance of having the right to vote and taking advantage of all the rights that were fought for by so many people.

I make sure that I do not take those rights for granted because so many people died fighting for them. My mother said that, if I don't like what is being done and how it is being done, exercise my right to vote. She never missed her opportunity to exercise her right to vote, and neither do I. She didn't have that right until she was in her forties, and I, until I was about twenty years old.

My mother lived her life the way she wanted to though some things were not her first choice. She did what she thought she had to do, but she did it her way. She didn't care what others thought though maybe she did and just didn't show it. She took life as it came to her, and she met life on her own terms.

I ask myself if I really knew her. I'm not sure, but I will say I admired her, not necessarily for what she did or how she lived her life, but I admired the woman she was, the courage she had, and the courage she had to endure all that. She endured a life of oppression and racism.

I admired that she took responsibility for her actions and gave no excuses.

I admired that she taught us how to survive, respect others, and be a part of a brotherhood and sisterhood. She made sure we had the compassion for people and knew how to help others, to have compassion and hope, to believe in a higher power, and most of all, to have faith. I could never have lived my life the way she lived hers. I sometimes wished that I had the guts she had. Maybe that was the lesson she was trying to teach me so that I'd be prepared for life's harder lessons. I feel it is only fitting to write about her and the other women of Bronzeville because there were and are many African American women like them with pretty much the same experiences—though not with the foundation the women I knew she had. I feel they are worthy of their stories being told, and maybe someone can learn something from their experiences. After all, they couldn't have been all bad, because look at me and my siblings and the children of the other women of Bronzeville and how we turned out. They made sacrifices for us.

About five years before my mother passed away, I asked her if I could interview her, something I had wanted to do for a long time.

But the relationship we had wouldn't permit it. After I turned thirteen, our relationship had deteriorated, and there wasn't anything rational between us.

As I may have previously mentioned, I resented her for many reasons. I hated her involvement in criminal activity and the things she had put us through: the drug dealing, the prostitutes and junkies in and out of the house, the police kicking in the door. The fact that she continued to have baby after baby, for me to take care of, drove the resentment deeper and deeper. I didn't know what to do with it. I was only thirteen!

It wasn't that I didn't love each one of my brothers and sisters, because I love them deeply. I wasn't allowed to be a child myself, and that is what I resented. I worried about each one of them as though they were mine. I knew that more than anything; I had become the surrogate mother of *her* children. This was a time in my life when I needed a mother. I was a child, but it was I who worried about my mother's safety. She should have been worrying about the safety of all her children!

I felt so deeply like she had betrayed me; I didn't know what to do. Worst of all, she didn't seem to understand that I felt she'd betrayed me, betrayed all of us our childhoods. She thought she was doing something to feed and clothe us. She thought she was doing the right thing; she thought she was doing right for everyone.

Maybe it didn't enter their minds, or maybe they were more concerned about their own survival than anything else. I guess, looking back from the inside out, I don't think they really understood any of it because back then it was "Do as I say do and not as I do." We were expected to follow instructions and nothing less. How does one see all the things we saw, what seemed to be the normal, everyday living, and not be affected by everything going on?

They had to know that it would have some effect on our lives.

I kept on asking why it didn't make a difference to them. Would it be any different if we had never seen anything else in our lives to compare it to? I wonder.

Even though everyone I asked said it didn't bother them, I couldn't understand why not. Drugs were an everyday occurrence in the Bronzeville I grew up in. We lost friends and relatives to drug and alcohol abuse. It didn't matter if you were outside playing or in the house, playing; someone nearby would be shooting up, someone was selling, or someone was prostituting in the building you lived in.

The smell of urine was so strong in the hall outside of our door, where people drank their wine, smoked their weed, shot their heroin. They peed themselves in the hall because they couldn't hold their bladders or move fast enough to get to a bathroom. We all peeped through the keyhole or stood on stacked milk crates to watch prostitutes having sex over the transom—a window that opened over the top of a door, which was glass. We thought our mothers didn't know, but how could they have not? There was no place to go, no place to run or hide from it; it was everywhere.

I had sense after the first time to not want to look anymore. Everyone called me chicken, but I wasn't. I had a conscience, and watching the private lives of others was nasty to me. Maybe it was because we were in the church all the time and I had guilt issues. I couldn't figure it out living in that hell on earth and going to church as though nothing was going on and nothing was wrong about all this; it was the only way we could escape.

It was all wrong and so contradictory to what was being taught to us at home and at church. Even today, I have issues with the church because they saw what was going on, and all they did was talk about it and made me feel even more ashamed and guilty.

I had nothing to do with it.

Watching women performing oral sex on a man and seeing the way the women were treated left a deep impression on me that there was no rhyme or reason to life. I couldn't stand it, but to everyone else it was fun; to me it was growing up too fast. I didn't want to know about these things, not then.

I thought it was wrong. My grandmother had the Ten Commandments on the refrigerator, and we had to read them before we could go in it, "Thou shalt not, thou shalt not" was always in my head no matter what was going on or what I was doing. When people I hung out with were doing something wrong, I was standing across the street because in my head was "Thou shall not steal" and

I would be in trouble if I got caught. I didn't want to disappoint my mother, my grandmothers, my aunts, and my uncles because I respected them, and I didn't want to give them anything to talk about. Though some of them had no expectations for me at all, let alone high expectations, it was a contradiction that others had these immensely expectations for me. I raised me in that hell on earth, so to this day, I have huge issues in coming to terms with the church after surviving the devil's reign of terror in my life.

Did I wonder at any time why my brother or my best friends shot up heroin? Did I wonder at any time why a lot of my friends were prostitutes?

I did. Why would anyone do this?

Anyone sane would wonder, but I was certain I knew the answer: if these were the only kind of choices you were faced with and it was all you saw, all you knew, every day of your life, doing the same thing yourself would be normal. I thought, if they were concerned about what was happening to the kids who lived with them and watched them every day, they would not do what they were doing.

I hated everyone and everything, and I wondered why God put us in this situation, why God allowed us to suffer like this. Wasn't anyone paying attention to our suffering? What the welfare people were doing was supposed to be a good thing. They were supposed to help us have the shoes, clothes, food, and things we needed to live decent lives. But that wasn't our reality.

I wanted to go back to the way we were living before, when we had structure and a routine to our days, back when we had guidance. We didn't have that structure anymore, and I became rebellious and angry, starting down a path that could only lead to my destruction. At that time, I was suffering from an undiagnosed case of what was known then as a "gross stress reaction" but now more fully understood by the name of post-traumatic stress disorder, or PTSD.

It's impossible to really describe what it took to attempt to escape the hounding of adults and peers trying to entice children to do use drugs, be prostitutes, or submit to the dirty old men who preyed upon the young girls in the community. It seemed like the only word I knew was "No!" I said *no* 150 times a day, if not more. Some days, they wore me down, and I would run home to my mother to escape so they couldn't get me. I would beg her to make them stop, terrified that I would fall prey to the madness around me. As soon as I was old enough to, I quit school. It wasn't that I didn't have good skills; it was because I was put down in school for being poor. There was the assumption that because I came from the neighborhood I lived in and the way I spoke that I should be placed in special education classes. The English I learned on the street and from my family was not because of the behavior I exhibited in the classroom; I wasn't a regular student. I was driven by the anger inside me and because I am Black. It wasn't very good to be Black back then because being Black was considered inferior. I was told by teachers I didn't speak correct English. Who would want to be in a place where you were not valued?

My mother always stressed the importance of getting a good education. Every day of my life, I knew that getting a good education was important, and I believed it as well. Being raised in the segregated North, it was far from easy to get that education. Living in the environment we lived in made it easier to hate school because they made me feel embarrassed and ashamed. I felt so different.

I didn't know anything about cultural differences, nor did my parents. I just knew we were treated very differently. If I had known there were cultural differences at work here, it wouldn't have made any difference. In my world, White was always right, and that made me ashamed of who I was; from their point of view, it seemed like I had no culture and I was irrelevant.

I had a culture, but it was always devalued in the schools I had to go to. My family members were always a close family with strong ties to the South. My first and second cousins were like brothers and sisters, and because of those connections to the generations, I had a powerful cultural pride. I experienced something that most people only wished they could have: the love of family, the love for my culture, and the love from and for those women who had once been slaves in my family.

The English I learned, I learned from them and my grandmothers. I grew up between the South and the North—between

Mississippi and Chicago—so I spoke what was considered a nonstandard form of English. My accent was from Chicago, but the dialect was Southern. I was part of the first generation in my family raised North. I was proud of who I was. I was proud of my family and my heritage. I grew up with people who were proud, moral, religious, and loyal to one another. I continued to feel that way—until I started school and found out I didn't belong there. My culture didn't matter in the schools. To them, I was nothing. Nothing about me or my cultural was taught.

I couldn't bring me into the classroom. I had to leave me at the door and become someone else.

Not possible for me.

That is the way I was treated because of the color of my skin and the way I spoke. I was made to feel ashamed of my family, ashamed the color of my skin, and ashamed of the way I spoke.

I didn't know what real prejudice or racism was until I began school. The teachers often commented on our lack of ability to speak in the way that normal children could so that they could understand us. I was placed in the special education room in the basement. The room had stacks of boxes, and the bare pipes hung exposed from the ceiling. Things that no one used anymore were stored there as well. The message to us was clear. We were in the special education room, which the other kids called the dummy room. The room, the attitude the teachers took toward us, and what the kids perceived us to be had a powerful psychological effect on me.

I felt so dumb.

I had to get out because I knew I was not dumb. I was criticized for the way I spoke and the way I wrote, and I saw nothing but red marks all over my papers. I wondered what was wrong with me that I couldn't learn the way they wanted me to learn. But I wasn't taught to speak, read, and write Standard American English.

My ancestor's original language—Hausa, Yoruba, Kiswahili, Igbo, and a hundred other languages—was beaten out of them and denied them the right to read or write. They taught themselves, and what came out of that was a different form of English one that slaves learned to be able to communicate with one another and incorporated their language structure into the structure of English. It was called Gullah—a form English African creole that Mrs. Evans spoke when she was disciplining us while sitting us.

There are words that have now become a part of the English language. One in, particular, is the Gullah phrase "kumbaya," which meant "come by here, Lord," a word used in a peaceful song that is asking God to be with the group that is singing it. Few people—if any—would recognize it (or admit to recognizing it) as a word taken from plantation slaves! And "mama" is also an African word that African Americans use to refer to their mothers, a word passed down from generation to generation.

I felt so inadequate and angry when I went home with bad grades. My parents would punish me for not doing my best. They said they knew I could do better. While that is true, what they didn't understand was that I was learning in an environment that belonged to someone else's culture and value system. Neither one applied to me.

They didn't understand that I was learning outside my culture, and what I was hearing was that we were all incorrect and dumb, my parents too. They didn't know about different learning styles. It didn't matter to them that what I was being taught did not apply to me or my culture or how we learned or what we learned. All they knew was the importance of an education for all of us.

I never had a problem with getting an education or learning, I just didn't know how they expected me to learn or what was so different about me. After all, I spoke the way my parents and grandparents spoke. When teachers told me I spoke incorrectly, it meant to me that my entire family spoke incorrectly. It was a put-down for me because I loved my language and I loved my people. When teachers wanted to meet with my family, I felt ashamed of how they spoke while, at the same time, proud of how they spoke.

Is it any surprise that I was hostile toward my teachers and my family members for making me feel that way?

I was being taught to be ashamed of my entire existence.

By third grade, I knew school was not the place for me. I did not want to feel this way in the middle of the tension between home and school. I felt as if I were not making my family proud, and I was feeling dumb at school.

No one understood that I was coming to a point where I felt that I had no need for either. I didn't want to be somewhere where I felt I didn't belong. I was coming to hate this place where everything about me was incorrect: my culture, the color of my skin, and the way I spoke.

I just wanted to be left alone.

As soon as I was old enough, I dropped out of school. The same day I left school, I promised myself I would return someday. When that day came, I would learn about what was important to me! I had a lot of cultural pride and determination even then though I didn't recognize it, and I was sure I would return to school someday. It was something that had already been instilled in me by my family. I wasn't the only one to leave school. It seemed like the whole neighborhood of young people dropped out, and many of them felt the way I did. I knew that, but I felt isolated at that time. I couldn't explain it, nor could I have done anything about it, so I left it all behind with a self-promise that I would come back someday.

Once I dropped out, I was on the street, hanging out, going nowhere, with nothing to do. Like many other dropouts, I was not content with that either. We may have lived in a place where we were all poor, but we shared what we had and took care of one another. We lived in a neighborhood with people like ourselves: we all spoke the same way, we had common understanding of what it meant to be poor and Black, and we understood what living in the ghetto was like.

We lived by oral tradition, or word of mouth. Just as our people did in Africa and as they did during slavery, and finally living in the rural South.

I am a mere two generations removed from slavery.

That common heritage meant that we had a loyalty to one another and a moral code of ethics. It's not like today, when kids kill kids and sell drugs to kids and no one tells about it. Back then, it was about being safe and staying alive. Today, it is about protecting the perpetrator rather than the innocent.

I started hustling pool, shooting craps, and pitching pennies with my brothers and the other guys in the neighborhood. I was good at shooting pool. In the fifties, there were few women pool shooters—I was the only one I knew of. Like the other women of Bronzeville, I did what I thought I had to do. What I knew how to do was gamble. It was a skill I possessed, and I was good at it, and it fit me. I still refused to sell drugs, use them, or let some pimp draw me in to be a prostitute. I had to survive some way, so gambling was it.

I was so good at shooting pool that I beat almost everyone I played. That didn't last long because the sore losers began to stick me up at gunpoint and take the money back. They claimed it was because I didn't tell them I was a pool shark. I did tell them how good I was, but they just didn't like the hard, cold fact that a young woman like me could beat them at anything.

I pitched pennies to the line for nickels and dimes since I was seven to make a little money to eat; that was something I did for a long time. I had to give up shooting pool because it became too violent and dangerous for me to play anymore except in actual tournaments.

I shot craps for a while, but I really wasn't into that game because it was violent too. I was good at it and lucky at it, but I didn't like it. I won enough money to feed myself and my siblings after my mother went to jail, but that was as far as I pushed it.

Even though I was good at gambling, I did it because I was biding my time. I was always trying to find a way out. I was not proud of my choices or the choices I had been given, but I was determined not live the ghetto lifestyle white people ascribed to us. I certainly didn't want this for my future children. Living in the North wasn't much better than living in the South with Jim Crow, but we had Jim Crow in the North too.

The questions I would have most liked to have asked all of them if I could go back would have been this: was it all worth it? Most of all, I wanted to know how my peers felt about how they were raised. Did they have any regrets? Were they as angry as I was?

There were many questions I needed answers to.

I wanted to interview those who were still living because many died young.

Some were teenage heroin addicts who abused their bodies and simply died, some were murdered, some contracted AIDS, some died of overdoses, and others were shot and killed by the police.

I remember a woman working for the *Washington Post* years ago. They published her story about an eight-year-old boy who was a heroin addict. The story turned out to be fiction, but when the story broke, I thought to myself, *She must be talking about a boy who'd grown up in my neighborhood.*

I thought no one was paying attention to her! When they said the story was fiction, I remember saying to myself, "It's not a lie, it is really true! She is telling a story from my life." We had an eight-year-old boy who was a heroin addict in our neighborhood. He'd lost all his teeth by age twelve due to his heroin use and died at age nineteen. I wanted her to know about him and to know about us, I thought at the very least she could help us tell our story, because no one else believed that such a thing was possible. I wanted her to know that she was right. It really did happen; there was really an eight-year-old heroin addict!

I never knew how to get in touch with her until she was interviewed by Ted Koppel for ABC's *Nightline.* I called the *Washington Post* and learned that she lived in Michigan, but I was never able to get in touch with her. I felt that even if the story she wrote was fiction for her, it wasn't fiction for us. It was a story that needed to be told. It needed to be dramatic to get the attention of others so they would know that there were children who were living in this kind of poverty. Others needed to know that the poverty caused people to fall into desperate measures to escape.

If she could have only spoken to me, I could have given her a story just like the one she wrote. I hope she will read this story one day and feel vindicated. For whatever reason she had lied about Jimmy, at least she would know there was a real one. It is not unique to me although at that time I thought so, but there were many neighborhoods like mine; she just brought it to the forefront.

The women of Bronzeville lost their children one at a time. One died because of six bullets from a police officer shot in the back. This was a common occurrence in any Black neighborhood. My brother's death was ruled "wrongful," and a lawsuit followed; we won—but it would never bring back my brother.

Another child of Bronzeville died of an aneurysm due to drug use. Others were murdered—not by the police—and another died of AIDS, sharing a hypodermic needle, and prostitutes, who, like all the others, were heroin users.

Some of us young people were lucky, or God had a plan for us—that is the way I would prefer to look at it. Even so, we did not escape unscathed. I lived with survivor guilt for many years, and every time I get a scar anywhere on my hand or near a vein, I hate it because it looks to me to much like a track mark; that is how traumatic the effect is on my life, living under these circumstances. I couldn't figure it out: why was I still living? We came along together in the same environment, yet people died all around me.

I knew there was something wrong with me because of the way I was feeling. I didn't breathe normally because I had gotten used to holding my breath when I was afraid.

I was afraid all the time. I lived with the belief that I was going to be the next victim. I thought I would slip and say yes to someone trying to get me to use heroin or trying to turn me out on the street as a prostitute. I was so afraid that I wanted to lash out and kill someone before they killed me. I thought that, every time someone approached me, it was to try to get me to use or do something I didn't want to do. I looked at everyone as if they were trying to kill me.

I was always on the lookout. I trusted no one and lived in fear every moment of every day. I didn't know what I was experiencing, but it had a name. That is another reason to be educated: so that you understand the things that are happening to you. I suffered from PTSD. I functioned that way for many years until my brother was killed and, six months later, I was assaulted and nearly killed.

My life had spiraled out of control. The only thing that had allowed me to move was fear. Terror had kept me functioning. But fear can only carry you so far. I reached a point where I was no longer able to function. The fear was not able to help me stay in control. For the first time in my life, I was losing control. I had extreme anxiety attacks, and I became afraid of my own shadow. I could not sleep at night, afraid of any little noise. Sometimes I would wake up in the middle of the night, unable to swallow, my left side paralyzed, my throat frozen.

When that happened, I thought I was going to die. I would get up in the middle of the night and run out of the door and just run until I calmed down and my heart stopped pounding.

I knew it wasn't just the assault, though; it was years of living in fear. It was years of being afraid of things like a police raid on our house and the police sticking guns in our faces, of police matrons sticking their fingers in my and my sisters' vaginas and in my rectum—to see if we were hiding drugs. We were little girls—seven, eight, and nine years old!

Through my teen years, the police would stop us coming from school and throw us up against the wall. They'd search us, and when they didn't find what they wanted, they'd harassed us. While this was happening all the time, people were dying all around us. Where were our mothers when we were being violated like this? Who could allow these things happen to their children? I went through many years of therapy once I was an adult. A car door could slam in the middle of the night and scare me into an anxiety attack. I would not be able to go back to sleep. I barred the doors and the windows all because of the memory of being assaulted in my sleep and in my bed. I cannot imagine a more horrifying attack—the worst violation anyone could experience. It was like being raped.

"I didn't do anything wrong" was what I said, all the time, day in and day out. At the same time, I would ask myself, "Why was I put here on this earth?"

I knew it couldn't have been for this kind of life!

When I was seven, I remember standing in front of our apartment building. I stood in the dirt, hair uncombed, wearing a yellow dress that tied in the back, no shoes, and looking around the neighborhood at the vacant lots and wine bottles and beer bottles all over the sidewalk. There was broken glass and dog shit everywhere. I clearly remember thinking to myself, *I know God didn't mean for me to live like this. I have to find a way out. I will get out.*

The place where we lived, Bronzeville, looked like some war-torn, foreign country. I am sure I'd seen pictures of Dresden, Rotterdam, and London in *Life* magazine. Everything was so quiet in Chicago and was so still at that moment because everyone was still asleep from getting high, partying, and shooting drugs the night before. This is not where I wanted to be. I wanted to be in the quiet of the Deep South in the country in Mississippi, looking at the grass and the trees and following the flow of the water running in the creeks.

I watched my friends die, and it seemed like there were ambulances on the block every night, with everyone standing outside, wondering who had died this time.

I am sometimes surprised I lasted as long as I did before my life went out of my control. I had been playing the game for so long—just trying to survive. I learned to manipulate everyone. I would do anything to keep from getting caught up in this web of destruction. Those lies and manipulations never hurt anyone; they helped to save me. I had to be a master at what I did; you could say that I'd had a superior education in playing a game of lies and deception, almost like deceiving the masters during slavery except I was deceiving the dealer and pimps and prostitutes. The problem was that it made me feel so ugly and so guilty inside. The lifestyle had become all too familiar to me. I was becoming someone that even I didn't like.

I needed to do something about it.

I had to face things and work through the anxiety to put things in perspective.

The next move was to get in touch with those of us who were still living. I wanted to interview them so I could know their feelings. Then I felt I could know how I would begin to process my feelings and get on with life. I wanted to receive much-needed validation.

Today

When I finally went to therapy and talked about a lot of these issues, I broke down and cried profusely in those sessions, something I needed to do for so long. I needed to understand that I can be vulnerable without losing myself or losing control. It felt good for once to relinquish control voluntarily.

Sometimes we think that we can trust again, but then someone can violate us again, and we just have to let go and move on once again, which isn't an easy thing to do. I had to learn to continue to trust blindly until someone violated that trust; then I learned to put that person in perspective and not allow that to make me mistrust the world

Many write about poverty or study poverty, but no one really knows what poverty is like or understands poverty better than the people who live in it every day. Poverty is violence, desperation, PTSD, drug abuse, alcohol abuse, and living by any means possible to stay alive.

I am talking about those who bring in the drugs. Poor people don't own ships or planes, nor do poor people have the means to buy the large amounts of drugs to put into poor communities. Those who sell alcohol and promote it by advertising it on every corner and do the same for cigarettes are also responsible for the biggest advertising in poor communities and are instrumental in creating poverty and poor health conditions. The people who were compensated by lawsuits were not the people in poor communities. Until people in power look at these issues, poverty will continue to be a nearly insoluble problem for the United States.

The culture before the Great Migration is also the culture today's Blacks know nothing about. If I asked young African Americans about their culture, they would not know what to say.

But what they do say is "I don't know." They will tell you they do not identify with their African roots.

I ask them, "How can you not identify from where you came from? These are your roots."

They can't because they have not been taught about the history of Black people in America, not in school and not at home. How can they gain cultural pride if they don't know their history or have a connection to the place from where their DNA originated? This is in part the reason our young people are so lost, because we are so disconnected from one another and our past. With all the oppression and mutilation of our men and women ancestors, brought here by force from Africa and doing, accepting, whatever they had to do to survive, they displayed all the courage in the world and did whatever they had to do to survive. We all should be ashamed that our children are ashamed of their ancestors and allowing others to make them feel that way. We need to correct the history books and not allow our children to disown their very existence. Not recognizing the courage and strength those before us had and taking pride in that. We will continue to have this disconnect in our communities and among our young people until they and we find their identity that lies in our past. What this denial produces are mistrust and a lack of self-worth. We should instead have Black pride and Black privilege. Black privilege is to know who you are and where you came from; knowing your history and being proud of it—that is what will close the achievement gap, instilling pride and confidence in our young people. They can continue to throw all the money they want at the achievement gap; it won't help until the curriculum changes to reflect the student body and telling the true history of this country. There will be students who are unsuccessful because it does not reflect who they are. This country was founded on "In God we trust," yet we have taken religion out of our schools. People have come from other cultures here for the civil liberties this country has to offer; they even pray in schools and anywhere they want to. This country needs to put religious teachings back into the schools and teach core values. It is not about denying others their rights. It seems to me we are already having the same issues here in this country that other countries are having over religion in their countries. The fighting and disrespect, separation of cultures, this should not be. Our young people are suffering, using drugs, committing mass killings, no concern for life. Why is that? Slaves were stolen beaten, maimed, drowned, all in the name of religion in the name of a god. Slaves were forced to believe in Christianity, yet it was the religion that set them free. The Middle East wars are doing the same things in the name of a god. We need to put prayer back in the schools. Our young people need to believe in a higher power. They need to know how sacred life is and who the creator and giver of life is. They need to have hope and faith respect for one another.

Our country needs salvation. Give the African American people our just due; give us that forty acres and a mule promised to our ancestors for the free labor that built this country. Until this is done, we can only continue to be divided. Find the integrity to do what is right for all the people. This country has never lived up to its creed of what it was meant to be but never was.

Why Am I Telling This Story Now?

I am writing about this because I think the life experiences of the women and children of Bronzeville are worth writing about. There were so many women who had been placed in similar situations as those of the women of Bronzeville whose story never got heard, told, or understood. Black women have been degraded, put down, humiliated, talked about, and disrespected not only by the system but also by some Black men who don't look at them as beautiful, strong Black women who have always been the strength behind them. The Black women, who have raised their children, stood by them, and the moment the Black men get on their feet under them, they leave, and guess where and whom they run to? Black women remain strong and are survivors just as they were during slavery, when they had to please the master in any way possible to save their men and children from being sold, beaten to death, or lynched. There have been a lot of sacrifices that Black women have made then and now for their families, only to be looked at with disgust and demeaned by the very men they sacrificed for, only to be called hoes and bitches by the hip-hop generation.

There are many children today who are in similar situations everywhere in this country. They suffer life without compassion, without understanding, suffer whatever life hands them. They cope as best they can. At some point, they should have gotten therapy to help them cope; some may have post-traumatic stress disorder as I did. But without treatment, they continue the same cycle in life from which they came. Then their children take on the same cycle—never knowing that there is something wrong with the way they live, not knowing there is anything wrong with it because it is all they have ever seen. They are never able to change their circumstances, never understand that there is another way of living, never knowing that they can have hope to or dare to dream of a world they too can have access to.

My hope is that this story will inspire someone so that they too can change their circumstances. Perhaps there should be children's books written for children who have had experiences such as this and who have PTSD. These books should tell about their experiences and ease their post-traumatic stress, something they can identify with just as I did with Hope and Help for Your Nerves, something they can relate to, and something that will give them hope. They need to hope and have faith that they can do better in life, something that inspires them and represents hope and a better outcome for their lives, something that will tell the stories of other people who lived and survived these same circumstances, people who had hopes and dreams that were successful in life. I can give this testimony because I escaped my life in Bronzeville. It wasn't easy, but I did it, and so can you. I am sure Bronzeville back then is not the new Bronzeville today.

All but one of my siblings made it out safely. It only takes one to raise the bar so that the others can see that it is possible to leap over it. It still haunts me today that my friends and family didn't make it. I always think, What if I hadn't made it?

How could it have turned out differently for all of us who survived if they had made it out?

We could have perished too, but I know, if I had not had the experiences I had, who knows what might have become of me? I reluctantly embraced those experiences. I have moved on, even though I am having an operation soon because of injuries I suffered from an assault thirty-one years ago. Learning strength, humility, patience, and faith led to my salvation. Everyone should know how poverty and drugs affect children's lives in which drugs and alcohol are the norm. It is a different world, with vastly different experiences, where they come from. These unique experiences can affect children's lives forever.

The problem with society is that we hide too much of the truths in life. Instead of loving and embarrassing, the reality of what life is all about. The good and the innocent, the shameful and the guilty, we tend to live in the confines of the shame and the guilt. We need to learn that it is not a sign of weakness to forgive ourselves. Then and only then will we be able to fully live our lives without the shame and the guilt. There are so many of us who can't make changes in our lives because we are carrying around so much guilt and so much shame, drowning in it. We continue to follow the same path, making more mistakes that keep us down.

Sometimes it isn't our fault. Sometimes we are put into situations beyond our control, yet we take on the shame and the guilt even though it wasn't ours to bear. It wasn't until I said to myself "Selling drugs, lying, stealing—none of those things were my doing. Why did I feel so ashamed of what and where I came from?" that I had to recognize this wasn't my doing. I needed to get over it and move on with my life. What my mother and the other women of Bronzeville did, they did because they were certain that they didn't have a choice. I did have a choice, and I had nothing to be ashamed of. It was that reality I had to reach and teach myself. I had a choice. I had not chosen to follow in their footsteps, though I am sure that was not what they wanted for us. I am sure that they wanted us to have more choices than they did.

This story is for those who have lived this experience and are still living this experience and who are not accepting the responsibility or the challenge of turning it all around. This story is for those who perished because they got caught up in the lion's den that Bronzeville had become and is for those who feel shame and guilt, for the children who are caught in this web and need hope for the future. It is for them to understand what it takes to change their lives, who shoulder the same shame and the same guilt, those who to live through it and became better people because of it. That is what it is all about, not only surviving and learning but also being willing to change the behavior, understanding that, to make a difference in their lives, they must change their behaviors. You just can't move to a new physical place and expect that your life automatically changes; it does not. You must work hard to change the behavior too. Your life doesn't change just like that; it takes work and a change of mindset and behavior.

It can happen. When we move to a new place and seek out the same environment and the same people, we wind up making the same ghetto we left behind. True, there is racism to account for in our lives, but as my mother once said to me, "Honey, you don't need no crutch because if you hate them like they hate you, then you will be no better than them, and that hate will eat you up. All you have to do is be the best person you can be." Once you have hope, education, and the belief that there is a higher power, your life will change. You don't worry about racism because there will always be someone who will hate, and that will be their problem. Those who hate live with their own emotions, and that kind of hatred destroys. Just as the Confederate flag was a symbol of hate, it had to come down. The flag was a symbol of keeping people in bondage; it was a representation to me that slavery should have continued. I won't live with hate in my heart because one thing I have learned from my mother and grandparents are that people who hate will destroy themselves—that won't be me.

People believe that changing places, physical places, in life will change their lives automatically, but it doesn't happen that way. You will have to change everything, including your friends, if they are part of the problem. This is another one of the lessons I learned from my mother before she passed away. They taught us common sense and prepared us for real life. But the one thing that continues to go through my mind is I would just like to know their mindset. Did they cry? Were they afraid? How did they feel about going to jail and doing time? Did they think the Mafia would retaliate on them if they told the police anything, or would they stand by them?

I knew they wouldn't talk because of the code of ethics—honor among thieves? Or was it because of the fear of what could happen to them if they did talk? I guess I can only continue to wonder about those answers. I know this it is not the life I wanted, and for those who live by a street code of ethics, those are not the ethics I live by. With all the murders being committed in urban cities, the killing of children and innocent people, and those committing those murders not being caught and no one telling who did it, you are allowing these things to happen. You can't come into my neighborhood and kill someone and I allow it and not come forward. I wasn't going to continue the legacy of the street code of ethics. I think we all had forgotten what and where the code came from. It was once used to deceive the master to save lives, not to cover up the taking of lives, to protect slaves from the masters, from being whipped, and from being lynched. It was not to allow the gangs to continue to kill innocent people or to steal what does not belong to them.

Poverty, murder, and this kind of life can bring on an undertow of events that leave one feeling helpless, invisible to the society in which they live.

These black women of Bronzeville became invisible indeed, and what made these women feel invisible was the fact that society refused to see them as human beings who mattered. These beautifully-born black women were feeling desperate, unseen, and unaccepted by the society in which they lived, but these women refused to go away. They decided that rather than hiding in a dark hole and succumbing to hopelessness, they would survive by any means possible. What made them invincible was they sacrificed their lives and their freedom to feed, clothe, and house their children. Apart from the wrong decision, I know my mother wanted to do right and was never contented with doing wrong. It was not how she was raised, and it was not in our culture. What was handed down to her and yet instilled in her gave was her courage to rise above it and come out on top. She lived her later years surrounded by her successful children and having everything she ever needed or wanted. She always said she feared God and never wanted to play with him. Deep within her, she always knew she must be strong to survive. The old-folk you would say, "Turn your mess a message. Turn your lemons into lemonade." Amid all her broken dreams in life, she knew what she wanted. In the end, she blazed her own trail, loved her family, helped those in need, and continued to believe in God.

Her culture, her family values, and our family history were handed down through generations of a loving family. In this modern day, many have gotten away from this notion, yet we *must* tell our stories of struggle and triumph, and others—often very misinformed and unaware of our plight will do it for us.

THIS IS WHAT HAS PROMPTED ME TO WRITE THIS BOOK.

What was passed down to me from my precious ancestors gave me the inner strength to have a voice, speak my truth, rise up, and be *visible*, rather than stay as the shy little girl that would be compelled to hide and fade away by all that had been done to her and all that she had seen and heard. It has made me an overcomer. It has made me an *invincible Black woman*. Deep within the core of my being are those values instilled. You too have your story. Tell it! Do not let it die with you! Do not just survive! You were made to thrive! And to those who left before me, RIP. You will never be forgotten!

The rich dialect that Portia McClain learned decades ago as a girl in Mississippi wasn't well-received at her school in the North. Today, she's looking for ways to make black English less of an obstacle.

She's hoping to build a language bridge

By Kimberly Hayes Taylor
Star Tribune Staff Writer

During summers in Jackson, Miss., Portia McClain sat on the front porch listening to her great-grandmother and grandmother tell stories about slavery, chopping sugar cane, baling cotton, picking peanuts and sharecropping.

She was enchanted with the richness of their words. So she asked them questions until her curiosity ran dry.

By the time they had died, they left her a precious gift. She had learned to speak exactly as they did.

When she was back home on Chicago's South Side, she thought little of the gift she proudly shared with friends, relatives and neighbors.

But the way McClain talked — with a Creole-Southern black dialect mixed with Gullah handed down from her African ancestors — didn't sit well with her all-white teachers in her all-black school.

The teachers always said, " 'Portia, you didn't get it right.' 'Portia, you are not doing very well.' 'Portia, why do you speak that way?' "

She asked no questions. Her papers were filled with red marks.

Turn to EBONICS on B6

Star Tribune Photo by Rita Reed

Portia McClain's graduate studies focus on the way black people talk.

Portia educates on Black English in hope of building a language bridge to a better understanding of the diversity of Black cultures.

EBONICS *from* B1

She's hoping to build a bridge to help black English speakers

She and the other first-generation migrants from the South were shipped to the "dummy rooms."

Those were the special education classes in the basement. She hated school. And she boiled with anger about her gift.

"I heard teachers say 'they' don't know how to talk," McClain said, "They don't know how to write, what are we to do with them?'"

McClain didn't know what to do, either. So when she turned 16, she dropped out.

She said it took nearly 20 years to regain her self-esteem. She went back to school at age 35 and began studying her language, black English, which some people now call ebonics.

Now she's 50, has a bachelor's degree and is at the University of Minnesota working on a master's that focuses on the way black people talk. In her undergraduate studies, she managed to get the university to recognize black English as her first language to satisfy a second language requirement. She found 172 books on the subject in the university's library and has studied black English patterns for 15 years.

She has gotten the attention of Minneapolis City Council Member Brian Herron, Minneapolis school board member Louis King and others. And she is determined to start an enrichment program that will help black stu-

dents in Minneapolis learn standard English better without making them feel inadequate or stupid simply because they speak differently from their teachers.

High dropout rates

The state Department of Children, Families and Learning is projecting that 62 percent of the black students in Minneapolis schools who started ninth grade in 1993-94 will have dropped out within four years. The number jumps to 67 percent in St. Paul schools and is about 62 percent for the state.

McClain, Herron, King and others believe those numbers are directly related to a language barrier between many black students and their teachers, who are primarily white.

How and whether to bridge that gap became a national debate after the Oakland (Calif.) school board announced last month that it would recognize ebonics as a language. On Thursday, the issue made its way to Capitol Hill, where a U.S. Senate subcommittee heard testimony on whether using black dialect can help black children learn standard English and whether the federal government should fund ebonics programs.

Critics, however, have argued that ebonics is not a distinct language. Sen. Lauch Faircloth, R-N.C., for example, said at the hearing that the decision to have teachers recognize ebonics struck him as "political correctness gone out of control."

At a glance:

Ebonics defined

The most well-known and widely used aspect of black English is vocabulary, which is in a constant state of change. As the larger society adopts words, the meanings of the words may change among blacks.

For example, the word "rap" has come to mean serious talk, as in "rap sessions," in standard English. In the black community in the 1970s, the word was used to mean talking romantically to win affection or sexual favors. In the 1980s and 1990s, it has been used to describe a popular form of music also known as hip-hop.

Some distinctive features of black English

➤ If *t* is the final letter of a consonant cluster, it is dropped. For example, "sof" (soft), "ak" (act). The voiced *th* is often replaced by *d*. For example, "dis" (this), "doz" (those).

➤ The invariant form "be" is used to denote habitual action or something ongoing. For example, "We be playing after school." (We play every day after school.) "To be" is deleted whenever one can use a contraction. For example, "He tired." "She at home."

➤ Multiple negatives are used in one sentence. "Don't nobody want no friends like that."

➤ The "s" is omitted when there are other words in the sentence that indicate pluralization. "I got two book." "He have 10 cent."

➤ Possession is indicated by position and context, not by the possessive marker 's. "Carrie hair pretty. "That John cousin."

Source: "Black English Dialect and the Classroom Teacher," Franklin Alexander, Medgar Evers College, New York City.

Portia sites examples of Ebonics and other misconceptions of students because of language barriers.

★ StarTribune

Published: February 8, 2012
Edition: METRO
Section: NEWS
Page#: 01AA

Gospel choir offers hope
Coon Rapids High School students recently started their own after-school choir, patterned after one in Harlem.

By BRYNA GODAR

The playful chatter and coughing quieted as the seven students formed a half circle in the classroom. Then one powerful female voice began to sing, "Wade in the water..."

Other voices joined in, creating beautiful harmonies, coloring the main melody with variation, yet sounding as one.

This unified sound comes from a new gospel choir of Coon Rapids High School students. For the past month, the students have been practicing Tuesdays and Thursdays after school, supervised by student learning advocate **Portia McClain**.

The idea for the group began when McClain watched a "60 Minutes" episode about a similar choir for teens in Harlem in New York City.

McClain said she had noticed a lack of hope and a lack of faith among kids at her school. When she saw the episode, she thought, "Wow, maybe that could help."

McClain showed the video to the Breakfast Book Club, a before-school reading group started in 2009 to foster cultural conversations. A few students liked what they saw, approached McClain and worked with her to form the choir.

The group has grown from three to 10—two boys and eight girls—and is looking for more members.

McClain said she hopes the choir can help kids find the faith and belonging she views as integral to success.

"I'm looking for some of those kids who are not having very good experiences, to try and help them turn it around," she said.

The choir offers a place for students to express their spirituality, to belong at school, and to sing.

"What I love is that we never forget the gospel in gospel choir," said Ekow Nana-Kweson, an 11th-grader. The members pray before and after practices and performances, holding hands in a circle as one student speaks. "We just give God the glory, 'cause he deserves it," Nana-Kweson said.

Marie Koon, an 11th-grader, said the choir gives her a sense of belonging. "I'm not very social with a lot of people in this school, and I'm shy to get into other stuff," she said. "This just makes me feel like I'm part of the school."

Sophomores Beryl Sang and Grace Kalala said they enjoy bringing their faith into all aspects of their life. "To have a gospel group helps us to keep that Christianity wherever we are, like in school," Kalala said.

"When you try to mix religion with school, you get into scary grounds sometimes," Nana-Kweson said. "It's a bold thing to be a part of gospel choir, because you're declaring that this is my faith, and you're doing something about it."

Nana-Kweson and others in the group are also members of Catalyst, a student-led Bible study at the high school.

Passing legal muster

Under the U.S. Equal Access Act, federally funded secondary schools must provide equal access for all student-initiated extracurricular groups, including religiously affiliated ones. If the school allows non-curriculum clubs, it must apply the same rules to all groups and provide the same resources, such as meeting spaces and bulletin boards.

McClain said her faith and church helped take her away from some of the hardships of growing up in the ghetto in Chicago.

"So many kids don't have that, especially today—they don't go to church, they don't have hope, they don't have faith," she said. "You have to believe in something, otherwise your life's gonna be stagnant, and that's the honest-to-God truth."

The group unanimously said the best part of the choir so far was performing at the Martin Luther King Jr. Jamboree at the Anoka Middle School for the Arts. They're looking forward to performances before the start of a track meet, at the spring show, and during the coronation assembly at their high school.

"They are amazing kids with incredible voices," said Annette Ziegler, interim principal at the high school.

The choir is mostly run by the students, some of whom have experience in school and church choirs. They agree on songs and then work together to arrange harmonies. McClain supervises and gives them advice now and then.

The students have been working concessions at high school sporting events to earn money to pay for a director. Joyce Davis, a member of the music group Sounds of Blackness, worked with the choir a few times at rehearsals. They're hoping to get somebody once a week to help direct and provide accompaniment for their voices.

"I think it's a bold thing that we're doing here," Nana-Kweson said. "I feel like we're doing something—something great."

Bryna Godar is a University of Minnesota student on assignment for the Star Tribune.

About the Author

Portia McClain was born in 1946 to parents who migrated from the Mississippi to the north (Chicago's Bronzeville neighborhood), in hopes of a better life. She was born at the very beginning of the civil rights era and was a teenager of the '60s movement, learning some hard life lessons out of poverty, oppression, segregation, and struggle. It was her sense of family and memory of her grandparents and great-grandparents and knowledge of family history that kept her strong and resilient. Her early educational pursuits were put on hold when she had to help care for her younger siblings. It was at that time that her paternal grandmother died suddenly in 1970 while simultaneously her mother was confined to prison. Portia is a woman of compassion; vulnerability, toughness, and wisdom, which make some see her as complex. She has for a lifetime opened her home to the rearing of children who were not hers. She has one biological son, Mario, as well as a host of grandchildren and great-grandchildren. The majority of them reside in Minneapolis, where Portia lives as well. When her siblings all finished school and she felt they were safe, Portia went back to school and earned her GED. She later completed her bachelor's and master's degrees in education. She is currently an adjunct professor and is a special education teacher with the State Board of Education. Portia's work as a student learning advocate has been featured in the local newspapers. She spent many years in Chicago, working as a supervisor at the University of Illinois and has been a part owner of lucrative small businesses.

Portia today, an Invincible Black Women Growing up in Bronzeville being Visible and transforming lives and instilling hope.

Portia has seen and survived many things in her life. She was in Mississippi in 1955 when fourteen-year-old Emmett Till was murdered for allegedly flirting with a White grocery-store cashier. Her uncle worked with Medgar Evers, the civil rights activist who was assassinated in 1963. Tragedy would later hit closer to home. The police shot one of her brothers in the back in 1981, and he died. Six months later, someone broke into her home, and the intruders chased her ten-year-old son out of the house. Portia has been beaten so badly by an attacker that it took thirty-two surgeries to repair her face because every bone was broken. After her perils of tragedy, she moved from Chicago to Minneapolis, where she started a new life and purchased her home. Because of the things she has encountered, she still has health challenges and is still overcoming them, but she has found a life of fulfillment and has touched the lives of many others.

CPSIA information can be obtained
at www.ICGtesting.com
Printed in the USA
BVHW071918140521
607265BV00008B/287